ASHE Higher Education Report: Volume 42, Number 1
Kelly Ward, Lisa E. Wolf-Wendel, Series Editors

Racism and Racial Equity in Higher Education

Samuel D. Museus, María C. Ledesma,
Tara L. Parker

Racism and Racial Equity in Higher Education
Samuel D. Museus, María C. Ledesma, Tara L. Parker
ASHE Higher Education Report: Volume 42, Number 1
Kelly Ward, Lisa E. Wolf-Wendel, Series Editors

Cover image by © iStock.com/rusm

ISSN 1551-6970   electronic ISSN 1554-6306   ISBN 978-1-119-20558-6

The ASHE Higher Education Report is part of the Jossey-Bass Higher and Adult
Education Series and is published six times a year by Wiley Subscription Services,
Inc., A Wiley Company, at Jossey-Bass, One Montgomery Street, Suite 1200, San
Francisco, California 94104-4594.

Individual subscription rate (in USD): $174 per year US/Can/Mex, $210 rest of
world; institutional subscription rate: $352 US, $412 Can/Mex, $463 rest of world.
Single copy rate: $29. Electronic only–all regions: $174 individual, $352
institutional; Print & Electronic–US: $192 individual, $423 institutional; Print &
Electronic–Canada/Mexico: $192 individual, $483 institutional; Print &
Electronic–Rest of World: $228 individual, $534 institutional.

CALL FOR PROPOSALS: Prospective authors are strongly encouraged to contact
Kelly Ward (kaward@wsu.edu) or Lisa E. Wolf-Wendel (lwolf@ku.edu).

Visit the Jossey-Bass Web site at **www.josseybass.com.**

Printed in the United States of America

The ASHE Higher Education Report is indexed in CIJE: Current Index to
Journals in Education (ERIC), Education Index/Abstracts (H.W. Wilson), ERIC
Database (Education Resources Information Center), Higher Education Abstracts
(Claremont Graduate University), IBR & IBZ: International Bibliographies of
Periodical Literature (K.G. Saur), and Resources in Education (ERIC).

Advisory Board

The ASHE Higher Education Report Series is sponsored by the Association for the Study of Higher Education (ASHE), which provides an editorial advisory board of ASHE members.

Contents

Executive Summary   **vi**

Foreword   **ix**

Acknowledgments   **xii**

Introduction   **1**
Racism and Racial Equity as a Framework for Understanding Race
    in Higher Education   10
Purpose of the Monograph   13
Outline of Monograph   14

Racial Frameworks in Higher Education   **16**
Foundations of Racial Theory in Higher Education   16
Critical Race Theory   17
Utility and Limitations of Critical Race Theory Scholarship in
    Higher Education   25
Racially Conscious Institutional Frameworks   29
Conclusion   37

Historical and Contemporary Racial Contexts   **38**
Historical Foundations of Racism in Society   38
From Old to New Forms of Racism in Society   44
Conclusion   48

Systemic Racism in Higher Education   **49**

Manifestations of Racism in Higher Education History   49

Racism in the Experiences of Higher Education Faculty   60

The Role of Racism in the Experiences of College Students   67

Conclusion   71

**Advancing Scholarship and Advocacy to Achieve Equity in
   Higher Education**   **72**

Advancing Racial Equity in Higher Education Scholarship   75

Advancing Racial Equity in Higher Education Policy   77

Advancing Racial Equity on College Campuses   79

Conclusion   82

**Glossary: Key Terms and Definitions Related to Racism and
   Racial Equity**   **84**

References   **87**

Name Index   **104**

Subject Index   **109**

About the Authors   **112**

Executive Summary

Despite decades of work to eradicate racial inequalities throughout society, significant racial disparities continue to plague the nation. One factor contributing to these inequalities is the reality that racism continues to play a formative role in determining access to opportunities for historically marginalized populations. Given that higher education is a microcosm of society, racism also shapes the experiences of these minoritized communities within postsecondary education. In light of the persisting significance of racism in postsecondary education, it is essential that higher education scholars, policymakers, and practitioners better understand the ways in which racism operates in policymaking processes and throughout the walls of the nation's colleges and universities. Such knowledge is necessary for policymakers and institutional leaders to more effectively address race-related problems on college campuses.

This volume is aimed at providing a much-needed synthesis of theory, research, and evidence that illuminate the ways in which racism shapes higher education systems and the experiences of people who navigate them. By centering and synthesizing research on the role of racism in higher education, we offer a more comprehensive picture of how racism shapes postsecondary systems and seek to help readers better recognize and understand how racism continues to permeate these systems. Moreover, we attempt to advance the conversation on what it means to work toward eradicating racism and advancing racial equity agendas in higher education in the 21st century. Combatting racism and advancing racial equity begins with recognizing that racism in higher education is not limited to overt racial hostilities, but is a systemic phenomenon that permeates institutionalized norms, policies, and practices that are shaped by a long racial history.

This volume consists of five chapters. In the first chapter, we offer an introduction that outlines the purpose, context, and outline of the monograph. The second chapter provides an overview of race conscious frameworks that have been created and applied to understand racism and racial equity in postsecondary systems. In the third chapter, we synthesize research on the critical historical and contemporary racial contexts within which higher education exists today. The fourth chapter includes a discussion of how racism shapes higher education policies, as well as the experiences of faculty, administrators, and students of color within postsecondary education. The fifth chapter offers recommendations for higher education scholars, policymakers, and practitioners who are interested in supporting higher education policy and practice aimed at advancing systemic transformation toward racial justice.

At both local and national levels, political and community leaders continue to wrestle with questions regarding how to make sense of persisting racial inequalities in the 21st century. While there are no easy answers to such questions, if higher education is going to truly live up to its idealistic role of promoting social progress and mobility for *all* students regardless of their racial backgrounds, we believe that they must abandon some of the assumptions that drive higher education policy and practice. Federal and state policymakers can no longer advocate for higher persistence and graduation rates without pushing higher education institutions to fundamentally transform and adapt to the historically marginalized and growing populations of color entering their campuses. At the same time, postsecondary institutions can no longer superficially commit to vague concepts of diversity, multiculturalism, or equality in mission statements and recruiting materials while failing to do the difficult work of pursuing systemic transformation to create more inclusive environments so that racially diverse populations can thrive. If we are to make significant advances toward racial equity in the 21st century, we must account for the systemic nature of the race problem in higher education, and develop more systemic solutions to it. Such work requires a coordinated and multipronged approach by postsecondary education leaders to advance scholarship, policy, and practice that focuses on achieving equity in higher education.

Most importantly, this volume is based on the belief that eradicating persisting racial inequalities in higher education and the racism that helps perpetuate them is a moral imperative. Indeed, while persisting racial inequities pose potentially devastating economic consequences for larger society, this monograph is based on the assumption that eradicating racial inequities, combatting systemic racism, and supporting communities of color that suffer from systemic oppression are critical matters in and of themselves. Therefore, we present this work with a sense of urgency and with a hope that higher education scholars, policymakers, and practitioners will recognize how advancing racial equity benefits all members of the campus community and larger society.

Foreword

The landscape of higher education has never been so diverse. At the same time, society has never been so rife with racial conflicts and racial inequity. As a microcosm of society, colleges and universities are well positioned to lead critical conversation about race and racism in society. The *Racism and Racial Equity in Higher Education* monograph by Samuel D. Museus, María C. Ledesma, Tara L. Parker leads readers to an ongoing understanding of the critical significance of race and racism in postsecondary education. The book posits that to further equity agendas, scholars, policymakers, and practitioners in higher education need to better understand how racism operates in policy, practice, and scholarship in higher education. It is important to recognize racism and its many manifestations before moving forward with equity agendas. Absent such knowledge, faculty, staff, students, and institutional leaders will lack the foundation they need to directly address race-related problems on college campuses and in society. The most well-meaning, well-funded, and well-planned programs can be foiled if difficult dialogues around the core constructs of race and racism are missing. The monograph helps guide the reader to think differently about racial equity by looking at the systemic nature of race and racism and how this shapes the conduct of higher education and the people who are part of the higher education community, both in general and within any particular organization.

There are many strengths to this monograph worth noting. In particular, the monograph offers an insightful presentation of demographic data that provides a foundation for the reader about race and social class and links between the two. The monograph offers an analysis of existing literature, identifies gaps in understanding, and provides a call to action. The authors provide not only insight and understanding, but also frameworks to guide practitioners in their pursuits to uncover and address systemic and persistent racial inequities. In addition, the monograph covers topics that have been somewhat undertheorized and serves as a replacement for conversations about why people "can't just get along" and why programs to remediate the situation often do not work. Without a systemic understanding of racism, well-meaning programs and policies can be misused or lack impact due to their lack of foundations in critical understanding of race, racism, and racial equity.

The monograph will be of great use and merit to scholars and practitioners. From the perspective of practice, the monograph gives language and offers recommendations to name racist practices and provide movement into equity. From a research perspective, the monograph provides a much needed synthesis and analysis of existing research related to different aspects of the role of racism in higher education. Theoretically, the monograph is also rich and practical. The authors provide critical race-conscious frameworks that have been used in research and practice. The monograph offers readers critical understandings of the theoretical constructs that have been used not just to understand racial inequities, but also to create communities where racial equity is present.

The ASHE Higher Education Report Series has been dedicated to critical examinations of diversity in higher education. We have done this by publishing monographs that look at groups of faculty, staff, and students who are from racial, ethnic, and cultural groups that have been historically underrepresented in higher education. We have also included monograph topics related to critical race theory and research methods that strive to provide conceptual and methodological grounding for research and practice that is inclusive of multiple perspectives. Underlying all these topics is an examination of the structure of higher education. To fully realize diversity and equity agendas in higher education necessitates critical conversations about core concepts and underlying challenges associated with racism. In this monograph, Drs. Museus, Ledesma, and Parker provide a much-needed synthesis on research perspectives, theory, and practice related to different aspects of race, racism, and racial inequities in higher education. When read together, these monographs can provide readers with theoretical and practical information to understand problems associated with racism, underlying constructs that help analyze situations from the perspective of race, and the ways that race shapes the practice of higher education. Further, all these monographs provide practical information and direct recommendations on how to acknowledge problems associated with racism and actions to take to create equitable spaces.

Lisa E. Wolf-Wendel
Kelly Ward
Series Editors

Acknowledgments

Sam Museus would like to thank his coauthors for their contributions, Christen T. Sasaki for her feedback, and Natasha Saelua for her assistance with the production of this volume.

María C. Ledesma would like to thank her coauthors as well as Dolores Calderon and Clay Pierce for their feedback and encouragement. Tara L. Parker thanks her coauthors and her graduate students (past and present) who helped to inform my thinking and rethinking of these important issues.

We dedicate this volume to those who tirelessly dedicate their lives to fighting intolerance, ending oppression, and advancing justice...

Published online in Wiley Online Library
(wileyonlinelibrary.com) • DOI: 10.1002/aehe.20067

Introduction

IMMEDIATELY FOLLOWING THE 2008 presidential election, many people perceived the victory by President Barack Obama to be a symbol of the ways in which the United States had transcended its long-lasting racial challenges and arrived in a post-racial era (Burnham, 2009). However, a plethora of evidence underscores the reality that *race*, the socially constructed phenomenon utilized to categorize people who share similar physical traits, is still a significant factor shaping the experiences of people within U.S. society. For example, since President Obama's victory in 2008, U.S. society has witnessed many high-profile racially motivated incidents and racially charged debates. During this time frame, the racial incidents that have received national media attention include, but are not limited to, the following:

- In 2009, a Black Harvard professor named Henry Louis Gates Jr. was interrogated for breaking into his own home in Cambridge, Massachusetts, and arrested, sparking national debates about racial profiling (Thompson, 2010).
- In 2010, the Governor of Arizona banned ethnic studies in Tucson schools under accusations that the Tucson Chicano Studies Program was anti-American, catalyzing national outrage and protest within Arizona's Mexican American community (Carcamo, 2013). The battle over this decision to ban ethnic studies is still being fought in the U.S. court system.
- In a 2012 racially motivated hate crime, a White gunman walked into a Sikh temple in Oak Creek, Wisconsin, and opened fire, murdering six members of the Sikh community (Romell, 2012).

- In 2014, a large number of alleged racial profiling and police brutality cases were recorded and distributed online, leading to rising racial tensions across the nation (Barrett, Vilensky, & Jackson, 2014; Davey & Bossman, 2014). These incidents led to protesters filling the streets to express their discontent with police abuse of power and widespread national media attention on racism in law enforcement and judicial systems.
- In 2014, national media outlets reported a rise in Ku Klux Klan recruitment efforts around the nation (Sgueglia, Marcellino, & Sanchez, 2014).

These are just a few of the many noteworthy racially charged occurrences in U.S. society that have permeated national media over the past few years.

Given that higher education is a microcosm of society, it is not surprising that racially charged events and resulting racial tensions continue to emerge on college campuses around the nation as well. In some cases, students of color and their allies have organized to speak out against these racial incidents at their institutions. Recent examples of incidents that spark racial tension on campuses include, but are not limited to, the following:

- In 2011, a University of California, Los Angeles (UCLA) student named Alexandra Wallace posted a racially charged rant on YouTube, in which she mocked Asians and Asian Americans using *"ching chong, ling long, ting tong"* sounds and disparaged these students for talking on their phones in the library and having their parents visit campus. The video prompted a backlash from the Asian American community nationally and at UCLA, eventually leading to Wallace leaving the university (Gordon & Rojas, 2011).
- In 2014, the University of Illinois, Urbana–Champaign (UIUC) hired Dr. Steven Salaita for a faculty position in its American Indian studies program. However, after Salaita posted tweets sharing his views about the conflict between Israel and Palestine that some found offensive, the UIUC Chancellor retracted Salaita's job offer just before he was supposed to assume the position (Hiltzik, 2014). Scholars around the country and both faculty and students across the UIUC campus subsequently spoke out against the decision, resulting in multiple national associations boycotting the campus, the UIUC faculty issuing a vote of no confidence

in their Chancellor, and a barrage of student protests against the administration's actions on that campus.

- In 2014, Northwestern University released a report indicating that one of its founders, John Evans, might be partially responsible for the notorious massacre of an innocent community of Native Americans at Sand Creek in Colorado (Northwestern University, 2014). Evans also helped found the University of Denver, where part of the campus community has organized to pressure the institution to acknowledge and address the racial history surrounding their founder.
- Over the past few years, several institutions, such as the University of California, San Diego, and Santa Clara University, have witnessed their students hosting race-themed parties in which students dress up as people of color using face paint and racist costumes (Museus & Truong, 2013).

These examples are just a handful of the many high-profile incidents that have sparked racial tensions in higher education over the past few years, and they signify the reality that college campuses continue to grapple with issues of race in the present day.

The ways in which race permeates higher education discourse are not limited to incidents that spark racial tension on college campuses. National conversations about the ways that race permeates higher education policy and practice also abound. At the policy level, in 2013, the legality of affirmative action at the University of Texas was first challenged before the Supreme Court in *Fisher v. University of Texas at Austin*, reinvigorating national debates about the utilization of race-conscious admissions policies in higher education (Resmovits, 2014). In addition, an increasing number of states are adopting outcomes-based and performance funding policies that have been criticized for disadvantaging colleges and universities with high concentrations of people of color, leading to increased conversations about the role of such policies in systemically limiting opportunities for already disadvantaged racial communities and perpetuating racial inequities throughout the system (National Center for Higher Education Management Systems, 2013). Moreover, the plight and fight of young men of color has been given increased national

FIGURE 1
Percent of United States Population Living in Poverty by Race

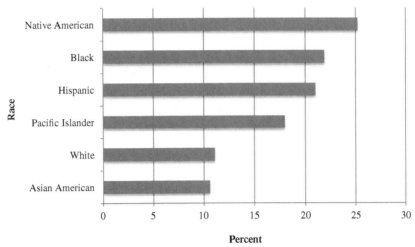

Source: Data are from the U.S. Census 2013 American Community Survey (ACS) Public Use Microdata System (PUMS).

Note: The sample was limited to those 25 years of age and older, and appropriate sample weights were applied.

attention by the federal government, regional policy arenas, and national media outlets (College Board, 2014).

A plethora of empirical evidence also indicates that racial inequalities continue to permeate society (Bonilla-Silva, 2003). For example, evidence indicates that people of color are more likely to be born into poverty than their majority counterparts. Indeed, in 2013, approximately 11% of Whites lived at or below the poverty line, while that same figure was 18% for Pacific Islanders, 21% for Hispanics, 22% for Blacks, and 25% for Native Americans (Figure 1). While Asian American communities exhibited poverty rates below 11%, which is a rate lower than all other racial groups, there are drastic disparities in poverty within the Asian American population. In fact, some Asian American ethnic groups exhibit poverty rates well below Whites and others witnessing far higher rates of poverty than the White majority (Figure 2).

These racial disparities in poverty have also been linked to racial disparities in health, with communities of color experiencing more frequent health problems than their majority counterparts (Centers for Disease Control and

FIGURE 2
Percent of Asian Americans Living in Poverty by Ethnicity

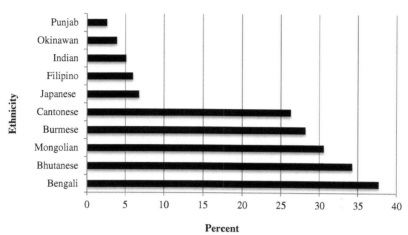

Percent

Source: Data are from the U.S. Census 2013 American Community Survey (ACS) Public Use Microdata System (PUMS).

Note: The sample was limited to those 25 years of age and older, and appropriate sample weights were applied. To demonstrate disparities, five ethnic groups exhibiting the highest and five ethnic groups exhibiting the lowest poverty levels were included.

Prevention, 2011). Indeed, communities of color experiencing high poverty rates have also been more likely to witness increased health problems and unable to access adequate health care. Moreover, this combination of increased susceptibility to health problems and lack of access to quality health care has been associated with higher mortality rates among people of color across the nation (Satcher et al., 2005). While President Obama's universal health care plan is now in effect, the extent of the impact that this plan will have on health disparities among various racial and ethnic groups remains to be seen. It can also be hypothesized that increased susceptibility to health problems and inadequate health care among people of color hinder their capacity to meet basic needs required to focus on academics. Moreover, decreases in the number of students of color applying to and enrolling in medical schools in states with affirmative action bans and the reality that White physicians are less likely to serve historically marginalized populations than their peer physicians of color raise concerns that extant health disparities could be exacerbated (Bowen & Bok, 1998; Garces & Mikey-Pabello, 2015).

FIGURE 3
Educational Attainment Levels by Race

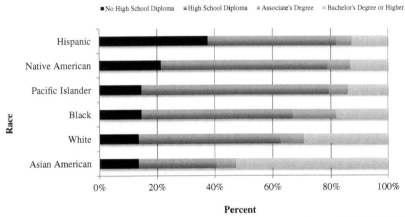

Source: Data are from the U.S. Census 2013 American Community Survey (ACS) Public Use Microdata System (PUMS).
Note: The sample was limited to those 25 years of age and older, and appropriate sample weights were applied.

Within education, racial and ethnic disparities are omnipresent, with people of color being underrepresented among those who attain credentials at every level of education. Indeed, national data from the Department of Education indicate that race is a divisive factor throughout K–12 education. Indeed, students of color are concentrated in underresourced schools, are more likely to be suspended, have less access to high-quality rigorous curriculum, and are taught by lower-paid teachers with lower qualifications (Rich, 2014). Not surprisingly, these inequities channel students of color on a pathway of decreased educational opportunity. Recent data show that approximately 13.5% of Whites have earned less than a high school diploma or equivalent, 16% of Black, 14.5% of Pacific Islander, 21% of Native American, and 38% of Hispanic populations (Figure 3). At the same time, approximately 29% of Whites hold a bachelor's degree or higher, while far fewer of their Black (20%), Pacific Islander (14%), Native American (13%), and Hispanic (13%) counterparts have earned a baccalaureate degree.

While aggregate statistics suggest that Asian Americans exhibit greater levels of achievement than other racial groups, these figures mask substantial

FIGURE 4
Asian American Educational Attainment Levels by Ethnicity

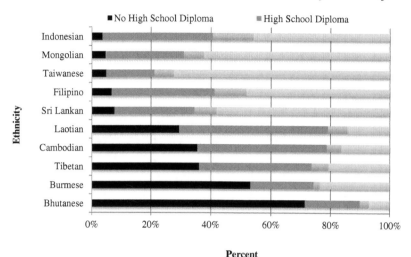

Percent

Source: Data are from the U.S. Census 2013 American Community Survey (ACS) Public Use Microdata System (PUMS).

Note: The sample was limited to those 25 years of age and older, and appropriate sample weights were applied. To demonstrate disparities, five ethnic groups exhibiting the highest and five ethnic groups exhibiting the lowest attainment levels were included.

disparities within this racial category. For instance, while over 95% of some Asian American ethnic groups have attained a high school diploma or equivalent, the percentage of Bhutanese (71%), Burmese (53%), Tibetan (36%), Cambodian (35.5%), and Laotian (29%) Americans who have been unable to attain this level of education is twice the rate of the White majority (13.5%) (Figure 4). Similarly, although some Asian American ethnic subpopulations attained bachelor's degrees or higher at over twice the rate of Whites (29%), other groups (e.g., Bhutanese, Laotian, Cambodian, Tibetan, and Burmese Americans) have earned baccalaureate degrees at rates far lower than the majority.

It is important to acknowledge that these racial and ethnic disparities are a national problem, and addressing them is a national imperative. Indeed, higher education policy researchers have noted that, if these disparities are not addressed, they could have devastating economic and social consequences for U.S. society (Carey, 2004, 2005).

FIGURE 5
Annual Income Levels by Race

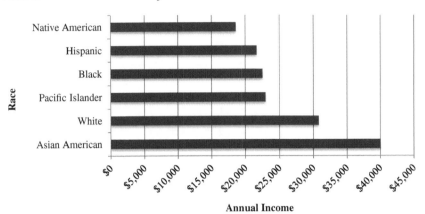

Annual Income

Source: Data are from the U.S. Census 2013 American Community Survey (ACS) Public Use Microdata System (PUMS).

Note: The sample was limited to those 25 years of age and older, income was adjusted, and appropriate sample weights were applied.

Given the continuing significance of race and racial disparities in postsecondary education, it is essential that higher education scholars, policymakers, and practitioners better understand the ways in which *racism* operates in policy-making processes and throughout the walls of the nation's postsecondary institutions. Such knowledge is necessary for higher education policy makers and institutional leaders to understand how they can address race-related problems on college campuses. Thus, this volume is aimed at providing a much-needed synthesis of theory, research, and evidence that illuminates the ways that racism shapes higher education systems and the experiences of people who navigate and function within them.

Not surprisingly, the aforementioned racial disparities in education are associated with occupational and income disparities in the workforce. In 2013, the mean annual income for Whites was $30,788, which was significantly higher than the mean yearly income for their Pacific Islander ($22,950), Black ($22,524), Latina and Latino ($21,656), and Native American ($18,596) counterparts (Figure 5). Although the median income among Asian Americans was the highest in the aggregate ($40,024), these statistics can be misleading. First, Asian Americans tend to be concentrated in the most

FIGURE 6
Annual Asian American Income Levels by Ethnicity

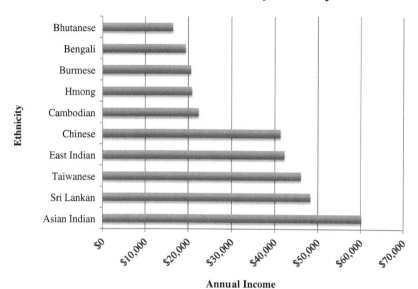

Annual Income

Source: Data are from the U.S. Census 2013 American Community Survey (ACS) Public Use Microdata System (PUMS).

Note: The sample was limited to those 25 years of age and older, income was adjusted, and appropriate sample weights were applied. To demonstrate disparities, five ethnic groups exhibiting the highest and five ethnic groups exhibiting the lowest income levels were included.

expensive geographic regions, meaning that they have a higher average cost of living than the national population (U.S. Census Bureau, 2010). Given that they are concentrated in regions where dollars have lower buying power, even if Asian Americans exhibited higher incomes on average in the aggregate, they do not necessarily translate into higher quality of life. In addition, when these data are disaggregated by ethnicity, several ethnic groups exhibit relatively low annual income levels. For example, the Asian American ethnic groups that reported the lowest average annual incomes in 2013 were Bhutanese ($16,453), Bengali ($19,383), Burmese ($20,659), Hmong ($20,887), and Cambodian ($22,442)—all of which were noticeably lower than their majority counterparts ($30,788) (Figure 6).

Unemployment statistics also illuminate significant racial disparities. In the third quarter of 2014, 6.4% of Whites were unemployed, which is a rate lower than their Black (11.7%) and Hispanic or Latino (7.3%) counterparts (U.S. Bureau of Labor Statistics, 2014). Again, Asian Americans (4.5%) exhibited unemployment rates lower than other racial groups, but such aggregated statistics mask significant disparities among ethnic groups within the Asian American racial category (Museus, 2013a, 2013b). And, when those data are disaggregated, they show that some Asian American ethnic subgroups have unemployment rates that are higher than their majority counterparts and the overall national average.

The disparities discussed above have generated an increased sense of urgency among policy makers (Carey, 2004, 2005). This increased urgency is partially due to the reality that people of color who face systemic inequalities represent a growing share of the U.S. population. In fact, people of color are projected to comprise over 57% of the U.S. population by the year 2060 (U.S. Census Bureau, 2012). Scholars have noted that it is likely that the aforementioned systemic racial inequities, coupled with these demographic shifts, will lead to severe economic and social challenges for larger society (Carey, 2004). While we agree that preventing the potential devastating ramifications of persisting inequalities is important, we also underscore that the importance of eradicating racial inequalities in higher education is often couched within this neoliberal framework to signify a sense of urgency, and we emphasize that addressing these inequalities is also a moral imperative. Indeed, the current monograph is based on the assumption that, regardless of the economic implications for larger society, eradicating racial inequities, combating systemic racism, and supporting communities of color that suffer from systemic oppression are an urgent matter in and of itself. In the following section, we discuss the importance of racism in understanding and addressing the aforementioned inequalities.

Racism and Racial Equity as a Framework for Understanding Race in Higher Education

Despite the significance of race, racism remains undertheorized in the field of education (Dixson & Rousseau, 2005; Ladson-Billings & Tate, 1995).

Specifically, there is a shortage of theories in the field of education in general, and higher education in particular, that sufficiently account for the role of racism in the experiences of people of color within the education system.

Prior to the 20th century, higher education research focused almost exclusively on understanding how best to serve an all-White clientele (Cohen, 1998; Karabel, 2005; Thelin, 2004). This focus mirrored the provincial view of the time, which was that institutions of higher education were designed to groom and prepare White "gentlemen" for entry into and leadership in civic and professional life (Brubacher & Rudy, 1997). Despite the racialized roots of higher education, it can be argued that most of the dominant theories (e.g., Astin, 1993; Tinto, 1987) that have been adopted and utilized by researchers and practitioners to study and understand the experiences of people in college settings have been deracialized and acultural (Museus, 2014).

Over the past half-century, researchers have made significant advances in understanding how racism shapes postsecondary institutions and experiences. First, higher education scholars have adopted and constructed useful conceptual frameworks that are designed to help understand and combat racial oppression (second chapter, "Racial Frameworks in Higher Education"). Second, many researchers have examined how racism shapes policies and the experiences of faculty and students in postsecondary education (fourth chapter, "Systemic Racism in Higher Education"). Higher education scholars have also stimulated discourse about how colleges and universities might begin to eradicate systemic racial inequities (fifth chapter, "Advancing Scholarship and Advocacy to Achieve Equity in Higher Education"). These bodies of scholarship are discussed in greater detail in the following chapters.

Nonetheless, despite the advances that have been made in understanding how racism shapes higher education, racial advocacy and the study of race in postsecondary education sometimes do not adequately account for the role of racism in causing and perpetuating racial problems (Brown, 1990; Harper, 2012). Indeed, even when postsecondary policy makers and educators seek to explicitly address issues associated with race, White racial frames work to diminish the significance of racism in their understanding and methods of solving racial problems. For example, Iverson (2007) analyzed 21 diversity action plans at 20 U.S. land-grant universities and uncovered how, despite good intentions, a historical legacy of racism and White supremacy undermined prodiversity policies and practices in postsecondary institutions. She found that, even when universities strove to promote diversity, many of them failed to recognize how their own institutional language worked to further reinscribe minoritized communities as "outsiders" to postsecondary education.

Race scholars have also exposed how higher education researchers fail to give sufficient attention to the role of racism in causing racial problems in higher education (Harper, 2012; Stanley, 2007). For example, one systematic analysis of 255 articles across seven peer-reviewed journals in higher education revealed that researchers who study people of color in postsecondary institutions retreat to majoritarian norms that ignore or dismiss racism as an explanation for the racial problems faced by historically marginalized communities (Harper, 2012). It is also important to note that the reluctance to name racism as a causal factor in racial disparities is likely not due to individually internalized White racial frames alone. Rather, researchers have argued that larger peer-review systems are permeated with dominant White racial frames and narratives as well (Stanley, 2007), making it more difficult for scholars to explicitly center the concept of racism, which is often considered taboo or outside the domain of valid knowledge. These realities underscore the critical role of professional editors and reviewers, who serve as gatekeepers of knowledge within the scholarly arena, in limiting or enabling researchers to utilize and center such critical race perspectives.

To address these challenges, the current volume offers a more coherent and comprehensive view of racial problems in higher education. In this opening chapter, we provided evidence regarding the continuing significance of race by demonstrating the persistence of systemic racial disparities throughout society and within higher education. As we illustrate, most significant social indicators suggest that resources, opportunities, and outcomes vary across racial lines.

Second, in the remainder of this volume we foreground the concept of racism as a conceptual lens that can be used to understand the aforementioned racial disparities. For the purposes of this volume, we define *racism* as a complex social system that functions to allow a dominant racial group to maintain power and privilege over minoritized racial populations, their conditions and experiences, and their access to opportunities and resources (Harrell, 2000). Under this definition, racism operates at a systemic level to privilege the racial majority's perspectives in the formation and interpretation of policy, the evolution of organizations and their environments, the construction of spaces on college campuses, the development and implementation of (co-)curricula, the delivery of information and support, and the internalized beliefs and perspectives of individuals throughout the system. We highlight how systemic racism contributes to racial inequalities by perpetuating a racially inequitable system of higher education.

Finally, we highlight how research on racial equity can help inform efforts to combat racism and cultivate more equitable postsecondary systems. For the purposes of this volume, racial equity does not simply refer to equal representation of different racial groups among those entering or graduating from higher education. We espouse a systemic definition of *racial equity* as racially equitable systems in which racially diverse perspectives are equally embedded in power structures, policy-making processes, and the cultural fabric of organizations (e.g., mission statements, strategic plans, curricula, etc.) at federal, state, organizational, divisional, departmental, and programmatic levels. We believe that an awareness of the nature of racism must be coupled with an understanding of how to advance racial equity to address higher education's most pressing racial problems. In sum, the current monograph aims to synthesize scholarship on racial inequalities, racism, and racial equity to paint a more coherent and complex picture of the racial state of contemporary higher education than what currently exists.

Purpose of the Monograph

Using the concept of racism as an underlying conceptual lens, we aim to accomplish three objectives. First, we seek to provide a comprehensive synthesis of literature on the ways in which racism shapes experiences of people in higher education. Due to the fact that a plethora of literature that is relevant to this topic has been conducted outside education, an exhaustive review of relevant theory and research is implausible. Therefore, we hope that the current synthesis and analysis of research primarily serves as a catalyst for ongoing discussions about how systemic racism shapes institutions of higher education and experiences within them, as well as how racial advocacy efforts can be (re)defined and (re)constructed to combat systemic racial oppression.

Second, through the current volume, we seek to take stock of the scholarship that has been generated on racism in higher education, so that we can identify critical gaps and areas that need to be addressed within this body of knowledge. Indeed, although a substantial amount of literature has been produced on the role of race in higher education over the past few decades, much remains to be learned about how these phenomena shape postsecondary institutions and experiences. An assessment of what has been accomplished and what goals need to be achieved in the coming years is useful in informing future efforts to generate knowledge that can help combat racial oppression in higher education and society.

Third, we provide a call to action for racial justice advocates and leaders in higher education. Based on our analysis and synthesis of literature, we provide recommendations regarding how higher education researchers, policy makers, and practitioners can go about addressing systemic racial inequities that permeate higher education. Our aim is to stimulate critical thinking about the racial justice advocacy that is currently taking place, and encourage advocates to rethink efforts to combat racism in postsecondary education.

Outline of Monograph

To accomplish the aforementioned goals, we present four additional chapters. In the second chapter, "Racial Frameworks in Higher Education," we discuss racial frameworks that have been applied to understand racism and racial equity in postsecondary systems. In the third chapter, "Historical and Contemporary Racial Contexts," we provide an overview of critical historical and current racial contexts within which higher education exists. This chapter highlights the deeply embedded nature of racism throughout U.S. society. The fourth chapter, "Systemic Racism in Higher Education," examines the ways in which racism shapes the postsecondary education system and experiences within it. Specifically, we provide an overview of how racism shapes higher education policies, the experiences of college faculty, and the lives of students in college. In our concluding chapter, "Advancing Scholarship and Advocacy to Achieve Equity in Higher Education," we utilize the information in previous chapters to construct and offer a set of recommendations for higher education policy and practice that are aimed at advancing systemic transformation toward racial justice.

Racial Frameworks
in Higher Education

S EVERAL RACIALLY CONSCIOUS FRAMEWORKS have been developed and applied to understand the ways in which racism shapes the experiences of people of color in higher education (e.g., Dowd & Bensimon, 2015; Brayboy, 2005; Delgado & Stefancic, 2001; Hurtado, Milem, Clayton-Pederson, & Allen, 1998, 1999; McCoy & Rodricks, 2015; Museus, 2014; Smith, 2011, 2015; Solórzano & Yosso, 2001). These frameworks have been applied to provide tools that can be used to illuminate the ways in which higher education systems can function to oppress people of color and understand how college educators and activists can more effectively approach diversity initiatives.

In this chapter, we review racially conscious theories that have been developed and applied in the study of postsecondary education. Specifically, we examine some of the most commonly used race-conscious theories in higher education discourse, including critical race theories and frameworks that highlight how racism shapes institutional environments and individual experiences within them. Throughout the discussion, we also aim to highlight some critical strengths and limitations of existing race-conscious theories.

Foundations of Racial Theory in Higher Education

As with all conversations about racism, history and context are important. In the context of the current discussion, it is important to historicize and contextualize the application of racial theory in order to fully understand its evolution and impact. Although the development and application of formal racial theory to the study of higher education is a relatively recent phenomenon, racial theory itself has a long, though complicated and often overlooked lineage.

In the early 1900s, W. E. B. Du Bois pioneered the study of racism in education (Winant, 2011). Indeed, Du Bois was among the first to apply a scientific method to the study of racism and education, including higher education. In his 1926 essay, *Negroes in College*, Du Bois wrote about the experiences of African American students in pursuit of higher education. He spoke bluntly about the challenges of African American students attending both predominantly "colored" and predominantly White institutions, noting that, "the attitude of the Northern institution toward the Negro student is one which varies from tolerance to active hostility" (Du Bois, 1926, p. 240). Du Bois (1935) also lamented the absence of truly equitable educational opportunities for African American students. He explained the following:

> [t]here are many public school systems in the North where Negroes are admitted and tolerated, but they are not educated; they are crucified. There are certain Northern universities where Negro students, no matter what their ability, desert [sic], or accomplishment, cannot get fair recognition, either in the classroom or on the campus, in dining halls and student activities, or in common courtesy. (p. 424)

Thus, Du Bois's work began to shed light on the role of racism in higher education in the early 20th century. In many ways, Du Bois provided a critical intellectual foundation for the contemporary study of racial theory and racism in higher education today.

Critical Race Theory

Since the late 1990s, critical race theory (CRT) has been an increasingly used framework in the study of racism in higher education. CRT has provided a revolutionary perspective for scholars dedicated to the pursuit of social justice within and outside of the law (Crenshaw, 2011; Tate, 1997). Borne out of the work of progressive legal scholars of color who concluded that legal scholarship did not give sufficient attention to the role of racism in shaping the legal system (Bell 1989, 1992, 2004, 2005a, 2005b; Crenshaw, Gotanda, Peller, & Thomas, 1995; Delgado & Stefancic, 2001; Lawrence 1995), CRT acknowledged in unequivocal terms that racism remains a central and indelible part of daily life for people of color living under a White supremacist regime. Matsuda, Lawrence, Delgado, and Crenshaw (1993) outlined six basic tenets to CRT that can be used to understand and deconstruct the roles of racism in legal policy and practice:

1. *Racism is normal:* Racism is an endemic and normalized part of American life rather than aberrant.
2. *Challenge to dominant ideology:* CRT challenges dominant claims of race-neutrality, objectivity, color blindness, and meritocracy, instead arguing that such ideologies are shaped and maintained by a White supremacist majoritarian structure.
3. *Sociohistorical context:* CRT challenges ahistoricism and insists on contextual and historical analyses.
4. *Experiential knowledge:* CRT also recognizes that people of color are creators of knowledge, including the use of their voices, narratives, stories, and chronicles.
5. *Interdisciplinarity:* CRT is interdisciplinary.
6. *A commitment to social justice:* CRT works toward the elimination of all forms of oppression as part of a broader project that strives toward social justice and toward ending all forms of oppression.

In 1998, Solórzano constructed a set of tenets that he argued are themes of CRT methodology in the field of education, and provide a framework more tailored to research and discourse in postsecondary education settings. These tenets are slightly different from those outlined above, and they include the following:

1. *The intercentricity of race and racism,* which suggests that race and racism are a central factor in the experiences of people of color, but they intersect with other forms of subordination, such as gender and class (Crenshaw, 1989, 1993; Russell, 1992).
2. *Challenge to the dominant ideology,* which refers to reality that CRT challenges dominant beliefs or meritocracy, color blindness, race neutrality, and equal opportunity (Calmore, 1992; Crenshaw et al., 1995).
3. *Interdisciplinary perspective,* which suggests that CRT in education employs transdisciplinary knowledge from history, ethnic studies, women's studies, sociology, law, and other fields to better understand racism, sexism, and classism in education. It is important to underscore that CRT challenges ahistoricism and analyzes racism in both historical and contemporary contexts (Delgado, 1984, 1992; Garcia, 1995; Harris, 1993).
4. *Commitment to social justice,* which includes the commitment to the struggle for the elimination of racism and other forms of oppression (Matsuda, 1996).
5. *Centrality of experiential knowledge,* which is the notion that the experiential knowledge of people of color provides legitimate and valuable tools for analyzing racial oppression and subordination (Bell, 1987; Delgado, 1989).

Although CRT has its detractors (Darder & Torres, 2004), it has managed to stake a strong foothold in legal scholarship and beyond. In education, Ladson-Billings and Tate (1995) and Solórzano (1997, 1998) introduced CRT to the fields of K–12 and higher education, respectively. And within the span of two decades, the use of CRT in the study of education has significantly and steadily increased (Dixson & Rousseau, 2005; Ledesma & Calderon, 2015; McCoy & Rodricks, 2015; Parker & Lynn, 2002). Indeed, both K–12 and postsecondary education scholars increasingly utilize CRT as a theoretical and methodological tool to analyze the complex dimensions of race and education.

It is important to note that CRT literature has, more often than not, been characterized by a Black-White binary (Chang, 1993; Gee, 1999; Wu, 1995). This *Black-White paradigm* denotes racial discourse that revolves around the experiences and material conditions of Blacks and Whites, while ignoring other racial groups (Espinoza & Harris, 1997; Gee, 1999). Although there is much about race and racism that can be learned from Black and White experiences, the Black-White paradigm also renders much invisible (Espinoza & Harris, 1997). For example, scholars have argued that immigration and language issues, which are central to studying the experiences of Asian Americans or Latinas and Latinos, are given insufficiently attention within the Black-White paradigm (Chang, 1993). Similarly, the Black-White paradigm does not center colonization, imperialism, and indigeneity in discussions of race, and these are critical concepts in the experiences of Alaska Natives, Native Americans, Native Hawaiians, and other Pacific Islanders. In addition, the Black-White binary does not adequately emphasize the value of analyzing relations between various groups of color (Johnson, 1997). Consequently, new emerging branches of CRT have been developed to move beyond the original Black-White binary to enhance the complexity of race discourse. These new critical race perspectives are not meant to supplant or contradict CRT (Yosso, 2005). Instead, these frameworks aim to produce richer and more focused analyses of racism in the experiences of various minoritized peoples and communities.

LatCrit: Latina and Latino Critical Race Theory

Latina and Latino Critical Theory (LatCrit) is considered a close cousin to and is based on the antisubordination foundations of CRT (Villalpando, 2003; Yosso, 2005). LatCrit emerged in the 1990s, and is focused on excavating the voices and addressing the concerns of Latinas and Latinos in racial discourse.

LatCrit scholars underscore issues that they argue are often ignored by CRT scholars, such as issues of language, immigration, ethnicity, culture, identity, and nation (Espinoza & Harris, 1997). In contrast, LatCrit asserts that race, sex, class, culture, language, accent, phenotype, and immigrant status shape their experiences of Latina and Latino communities (Yosso, 2005; Yosso, Parker, Solórzano, & Lynn, 2004). For example, LatCrit scholars insist, "questions of language, culture and nation are inextricably intertwined with questions of race" (Espinoza & Harris, 1997, p. 499). As such, researchers depend on LatCrit to investigate how such unique indicators shape and influence educational opportunities for Latina and Latino students (Huber, 2009; Huber & Malagon, 2006; Solórzano & Delgado Bernal, 2001; Solórzano & Yosso, 2001; Villalpando, 2004).

TribalCrit: Tribal Critical Race Theory

Tribal Critical Theory (TribalCrit) emerged in the field of education and as a result of the need for a critical framework that better acknowledged and centered Native American histories and realities (Brayboy, 2005). TribalCrit is founded on CRT and rooted in the diverse and nuanced epistemologies and ontologies that exist within Indigenous communities.

Unlike LatCrit scholars, who have primarily applied CRT to center issues most relevant to this population in the study of Latina and Latino experiences with racism, TribalCrit scholars have developed and applied a distinct framework tailored to Indigenous populations. Brayboy developed a TribalCrit framework that includes nine distinct features:

1. Colonization is endemic to society.
2. U.S. policies toward Indigenous populations are founded on imperialism, White supremacy, and a desire for material gain.
3. Indigenous communities occupy a liminal space, both politically and racially.
4. Indigenous populations seek tribal sovereignty, tribal autonomy, self-determination, and self-identification.
5. Culture, knowledge, and power assume new meanings when viewed from an Indigenous perspective.
6. Government and education policies are aimed at advancing the problematic goal of assimilation of Indigenous communities.
7. Tribal philosophies, beliefs, customs, traditions, and visions are essential to understanding the lived realities of Indigenous peoples.
8. Stories comprise theory and are legitimate sources of data.
9. Theory and practice are interconnected, and scholars must work toward social change.

Thus, TribalCrit honors Indigenous ways of knowing, acknowledges the role of colonization and imperialism in shaping the experience of Indigenous peoples, and emphasizes exposing systems that oppress indigenous peoples and improve these communities (Brayboy, 2005). Scholars have begun to apply a TribalCrit lens to critically examine how colleges and universities embrace celebrations of superficial forms of multiculturalism but reinforce systems of racial oppression that harm Indigenous populations (Castagno & Lee 2007; Covarrubias & Windchief, 2009; Wright & Balutski, 2013). For example, they argue that postsecondary institutions' use of Native American mascots do nothing to "honor" Native Americans and instead represents an exercise in White supremacy.

AsianCrit: Asian Critical Race Theory

Asian Critical Race Theory (AsianCrit) acknowledges that Asians and Asian Americans experience unique forms of racism in U.S. society (Buenavista, Jayakumar, & Misa-Escalante, 2009; Chang, 1993; Liu, 2009; Museus, 2013b; Museus & Iftikar, 2014). AsianCrit research focuses on dismantling stereotypes of Asians and Asian Americans, illuminates how historic and contemporary forms of racism shape their experiences, and gives voice to their unique experiences. And, scholars have used CRT to analyze the experiences of Asians and Asian Americans in higher education specifically (Buenavista & Chen, 2013; Buenavista et al., 2009; Museus, 2013b; Museus & Saelua, 2014; Teranishi, Behringer, Grey, and Parker, 2009). Much of this research aims to debunk the model minority myth, or the stereotype that all Asians and Asian Americans achieve universal and unparalleled academic success, by illuminating the ways in which racism creates challenges for this population and excavating their authentic voices in the context of higher education systems.

Based on the notion that a framework more tailored to Asian Americans might help advance AsianCrit scholarship and building on the work of previous CRT and Asian American Studies scholars (e.g., Buenavista & Chen, 2013; Buenavista et al., 2009; Chan, 1991; Chon, 1995; Crenshaw, 1993; Espiritu, 2008; Matsuda, 1996; Museus & Kiang, 2009; Saito, 1997; Sue, Bucceri, Lin, Nadal, & Torino, 2007; Takaki, 1989; Umemoto, 1989; Yu, 2006), Museus and Iftikar (2014) outlined seven tenets of an AsianCrit framework. Similar to the TribalCrit framework, the AsianCrit tenets provide a more nuanced lens that scholars can use to analyze the impact of racism and other forms of oppression on Asian and Asian American experiences:

1. *Asianization* suggests that AsianCrit, like original CRT frameworks, is based on the notion that nativistic racism is a pervasive aspect of Western society, but also assumes that society racializes Asian Americans in distinct ways that treat them as a monolithic group of overachieving model minorities, perpetual foreigners, and threatening yellow perils, emasculated men, and sexually exoticized and objectified women.

2. *Transnational contexts* underscores the value of historical and contemporary national contexts, but also centers the notion that international histories, events, processes, migrations, and the like have a profound impact on the experiences of Asian Americans.

3. *(Re)Constructive history* is based on the reality that Asian Americans are largely invisible and voiceless in American history and underscores the importance of constructing a collective Asian American historical narrative that includes the voices and contributions of Asian American U.S. society.

4. *Strategic (anti)essentialism* emphasizes that dominant oppressive economic, political, and social forces shape the ways in which Asian Americans are racialized in society, but also acknowledges that Asian Americans also can and do engage in political alliances and actions that shape these processes.

5. *Intersectionality* is similar to the intersectionality tenet of CRT and based on the reality that racism and other forms of oppression (e.g., imperialism, sexism, genderism, heterosexism, ableism, etc.) mutually shape Asian American realities.

6. *Story, theory, and praxis* combines tenets of CRT and TribalCrit to underscore the notion that Asian American stories, theory, and practice are all inextricably intertwined elements in the analysis of Asian American experiences and advocacy for Asian American communities.

7. *Commitment to social justice* underscores the notion that AsianCrit is dedicated to advocating for the end of all forms of oppression.

Thus, AsianCrit perspectives emphasize elements of a critical framework that are not typically the focus of CRT scholarship and discourse, but are essential in understanding the experiences of Asians and Asian Americans. These include the unique ways in which Asians and Asian Americans are racialized in U.S. society, the role of international contexts, and the importance of constructing a historical narrative that includes Asian American voices. AsianCrit perspectives underscore the value and interconnectedness of theory and practice, similar to TribalCrit, but also underscore their relationships to Asian and Asian American stories.

KānakaCrit: Native Hawaiian Critical Theory

Native Hawaiians occupy a unique place in racial discourse. Although Native Hawaiians are often lumped into the same category as Asian Americans or other Pacific Islanders, they have a history that is very different than their Asian American counterparts. As discussed above, the colonization of Hawaii plays a critical role in shaping the current conditions of the Native Hawaiian community and their identities and experiences. As such, TribalCrit has been used as a tool to analyze the experiences of Native Hawaiians (Wright & Balutski, 2013).

Although TribalCrit has been used to analyze the experiences of Native Hawaiians, it could be argued that this perspective does not holistically capture the realities of Native Hawaiians (Reyes, 2014). Therefore, building on the work of previous CRT, higher education, and indigenous scholars (Brayboy, 2005; Dudley, 1990; Ho'omanawanui, 2004; Kame'eleihiwa, 1992; Ladson-Billings, 2009; Meyer, 2008; Museus & Iftikar, 2014; Solórzano & Yosso, 2009), Reyes (2014) has constructed a KānakaCrit framework that is based on Hawaiian epistemologies and centers issues of colonialism, sovereignty, liminality, social justice, and survivance (i.e., Native survival and resistance) in that perspective (Vizenor, 2008; Vizenor & Lee, 1999). This KānakaCrit framework includes the following five tenets:

1. Occupation and colonialism are endemic to society.
2. 'Ōiwi (i.e., Native Hawaiian) identities are multiple, intersecting, and liminal.

3. Social justice is inherently tied to Native Hawaiian ea (i.e., sovereignty, life, and breath) and the lāhui (i.e., nation or people).
4. KanakaCrit works toward social justice and restoring pono (i.e., balance and harmony).
5. As Native Hawaiians learn to tell their moʻolelo (i.e., histories or stories), they contribute to their survivance (i.e., native survival and resistance).

Reyes (2014) notes that she purposefully does not italicize Hawaiian words embedded in the tenets as a form of resistance to the assumption that Hawaiian language is linguistically foreign. The KanakaCrit framework is another example of the ways in which scholars have adapted CRT perspectives to better fit their communities and to better illuminate the experiences of often-invisible populations in higher education discourse.

Utility and Limitations of Critical Race Theory Scholarship in Higher Education

CRT perspectives have been utilized in higher education research and discourse for multiple purposes. First, CRT scholarship in postsecondary education has functioned to illuminate the voices of people of color within academia (e.g., Bonner et al., 2014; Espino, Muñoz, & Kiyama, 2010; Solórzano, 1998; Solórzano, Ceja, & Yosso, 2000). In this way, CRT scholars have challenged notions of U.S. society being in a color-blind era and institutions of higher education being free of significant racial problems.

Second, CRT scholarship in higher education underscores the reality that historical and social contexts influence postsecondary systems and experiences within them. Indeed, the very land on which many of the nation's colleges and universities stand often reflects a bloody history of racial domination and conquest, and scholars have documented how slave labor and the dispossession of Native Americans were crucial factors in building some of the nation's most elite private colleges (Wilder, 2013). Others have illuminated the nature of racialized space on college campuses that privilege the White majority and marginalize people of color (Brown-Nagin, Guinier, & Torres, 2015;

Muñoz, 2009). Researchers have also noted that White people founded many of the nation's postsecondary institutions to serve White students (Brown-Nagin et al., 2015). Today, the remnants of this racist past have very real effects on current college students. For example, some campuses in the South house a landscape that includes statues and buildings in honor of Confederate Civil War heroes and espoused segregationists, which are symbols that continue to send signals to minoritized students that their racial subjugation is a celebrated element of these institutions' historical past.

Third, higher education scholars have employed CRT to deconstruct dominant discourse in postsecondary education (McCoy & Rodricks, 2015). For example, CRT has been used to combat prevailing deficit-oriented frameworks of historically minoritized students of color. Dominant deficit paradigms perpetuate perceptions of people of color as inherently inferior in status, intelligence, and standing to Whites by focusing on failure as a result of the dispositions of students of color while ignoring how systemic factors shape their educational opportunities and outcomes (Valencia, 1997). These dominant deficit frames also privilege White values and norms in education discourse, and can therefore influence policy and program development, interpretation, and implementation in ways that disadvantage people of color (Brown, 1990; Tate, 1997). Therefore, CRT scholars have challenged these dominant narratives by reframing conversations about educational opportunity and outcomes in less deficit-oriented ways (e.g., Yosso, 2005).

Similarly, through critical race analyses, higher education researchers have problematized such concepts of meritocracy and color blindness (Carter Andrews & Tuitt, 2013). The concepts of meritocracy and color blindness are ubiquitous in postsecondary research and discourse. Critical race scholars have uncovered how critics of race-conscious educational policy often champion meritocracy and color blindness to defend dominant views and values that function to subordinate people of color. CRT excavates the racism that is inherent in such linchpins of dominant ideologies and democratic discourse by unmasking how they, either consciously or unconsciously, camouflage or uphold White power and privilege (Iverson, 2007).

Fourth, a small and growing body of scholarship utilizes CRT as a lens to illuminate the ways in which higher education policy can reinforce systems of racial oppression. Specifically, scholars have used CRT to explain that education policy that is viewed as a rational process targeted at positive change often restructures and reinforces racial inequity (Gillborn, 2005; Iverson, 2007), how racial hierarchies manifest in admissions processes to perpetuate racial inequity (Yosso, Parker, Solórzano, & Lynn, 2004), how racism permeates faculty promotion and retention processes (Delgado Bernal & Villalpando, 2002; Patton, 2004; Patton & Catching, 2009; Stanley, 2006), and how dominant narratives permeate organizational culture to disadvantage minoritized populations (Museus, Ravello, & Vega, 2012). In sum, scholars have begun to utilize CRT to illuminate how higher education policies can mask and sustain racism within the academy, but this body of research is only just emerging within the field.

Finally, researchers have used CRT to expose how racism permeates the lived experience of people of color in higher education and to give voice to the experiences of those historically silenced and marginalized. Scholars have applied CRT to study the experiences of people of color within hostile campus racial climates, as well as the academic and psychological effects that result from such environments (e.g., Gildersleeve, Croom, & Vasquez, 2011; Gusa, 2010; Harper, 2009; Jayakumar, Howard, Allen, & Han, 2009; Museus, Ravello, et al., 2012; Smith, Allen, & Danley, 2007; Solórzano, 1998; Solórzano et al., 2000; Truong & Museus, 2012; Villalpando, 2003). As such, CRT has enabled postsecondary scholars in higher education to name racism as a systemic reality that shapes the experiences of people of color within postsecondary institutions (Ledesma & Solórzano, 2013).

Like all theoretical frameworks, CRT also has limitations and has been employed, in limited ways, to the study of higher education thus far. First, it is important to acknowledge that CRT is not a panacea for analyzing, understanding, and eradicating racial problems. While CRT has substantial utility to shed light on the ways in which racism shapes higher education and experiences within it, it can be argued that CRT tenets are less effective at providing higher education policy makers and college educators with race-conscious explanations of what ideal postsecondary institutional environments should look like or how postsecondary educators can navigate the process of advocating for racial justice by transforming higher education institutions.

For example, CRT frameworks do not provide a race-conscious framework for understanding how to maximize student success among diverse populations or how to navigate the racial politics of an institution in equity efforts. Race-conscious frameworks that explain such educational processes are also crucial in efforts to not only concretizing an understanding of how racism works, but also utilizing that knowledge to (re)think, (re)analyze, and (re)define common educational processes.

Second, as mentioned, original CRT frameworks and their tenets do not always adequately capture the conditions and realities of populations that are marginalized within racial discourse. While branches of CRT have been developed to highlight these situations and experiences (e.g., Brayboy, 2005; Museus & Iftikar, 2014; Reyes, 2014), these descendant CRT perspectives have only been minimally utilized in the study of higher education. This reality could be due to many reasons, including the fact that they are relatively new and there are comparatively few scholars studying the populations to which they apply in the field of postsecondary education. Thus, it could be argued that the extent to which CRT illuminates the voices and knowledge of some populations of color (e.g., non-Native Hawaiian Pacific Islanders, multiracial populations, etc.) remains drastically limited within this discourse. Therefore, the increased application of CRT perspectives to study these groups is warranted.

Third, research that applies CRT to study important topics in higher education, such as college leadership or the economics of higher education, is difficult to find. Moreover, while researchers have utilized CRT to illuminate the voices of people of color in substantial ways (McCoy & Rodricks, 2015), new critiques of the ways in which complex systemic racism shapes seemingly objective educational policies, programs, and practices are less prevalent. CRT perspectives, for example, have much potential analytical power in the analysis of performance funding mechanisms, financial aid policies, institutional strategic plans, institutional cultures, promotion and tenure systems, institutional stratification and the disproportionate influx of resources to the most selective institutions, to name a few (Museus, Ravello, et al., 2012). Thus, more analyses that apply CRT to deconstruct such complex policies and practices are needed.

Racially Conscious Institutional Frameworks

It is important to acknowledge that CRT perspectives are not the only conceptual frameworks that have been offered to analyze, better understand, and address racism and racial equity within the postsecondary education system. Higher education researchers have developed models that offer an understanding of campus environments, illuminate the complex and multifaceted nature of institutional efforts to move toward racial equity, outline what is needed to construct equitable institutions, and delineate processes for achieving racial equity. It could be argued that the racially conscious institutional frameworks that we discuss herein focus less on explicitly naming, exposing, challenging, and critiquing systems of racial oppression than CRT. Nevertheless, we believe that these frameworks respond to institutional racism in important ways. The frameworks are founded on assumptions that racism permeates institutions of higher education and leads to environments that disadvantage marginalized populations. These racially conscious institutional models attempt not only to shed additional light on how racism permeates and manifests in various aspects of postsecondary campuses, but also to offer perspectives that can guide collective action to combat systemic racism and racial inequity. Therefore, they are essential to developing a holistic understanding of racism in higher education and how to address it.

In this section, we review some of these racially conscious frameworks. While a comprehensive review of racially conscious models that are utilized in higher education research and discourse is beyond the scope of this volume, we provide an overview of four frameworks that, together, we believe offer a relatively comprehensive overview of current discourse on systemic racism and racial equity within institutions of higher education.

The Campus Climate for Diversity Framework

A substantial and growing body of scholarship analyzes the ways in which campus racial climates shape the experiences of students of color in postsecondary education (Hurtado et al., 1998, 1999; Museus, Nichols, & Lambert, 2008). This body of literature illuminates how students of color report more negative experiences within the campus climate and how hostile climates can lead to more negative outcomes (e.g., sense of belonging or persistence and degree completion) (Hurtado & Carter, 1997; Locks, Hurtado, Bowman, & Oseguera, 2008; Museus et al., 2008). Higher education researchers have also shed light on *how* college students of color experience hostility in the campus racial climate, which is a body of literature that we review more thoroughly in the fourth chapter, "Systemic Racism in Higher Education."

The campus racial climate can be defined in a variety of ways (Bauer, 1998; Hurtado et al., 1999; Solórzano et al., 2000). Hurtado et al. (1999) defined the campus racial climate as a part of the institutional environment that encompasses campus community members' attitudes, perceptions, behaviors, and expectations with regard to issues of race, ethnicity, and diversity. Hurtado et al. (1998, 1999) have offered arguably the most highly visible, comprehensive, and widely used campus racial climate framework that describes campus racial climate as a multidimensional construct. The climate framework takes into account the ways in which forces that are external to the institution, such as governmental policy and sociohistorical context, influence institutions' racial climate. Higher education researchers, however, have given most of their attention to the factors that exist within and are under the control of U.S. colleges and universities (Hurtado, Alvarez, Guillermo-Wann, & Cuellar, 2012). These factors include the compositional or structural diversity of college campuses, psychological dimension of the climate, behavioral dimension of the climate, and history and legacy of inclusion or exclusion of various racial groups at postsecondary institutions (Hurtado et al., 1998, 1999).

The campus racial climate for diversity framework underscores the complexity of the concept of institutional racial climate, while also constituting a model that outlines specific factors that influence the climate and can be the focus of diversity efforts. For example, the model suggests that postsecondary campuses can address their institutions' legacy of excluding marginalized populations, increasing structural diversity (i.e., admitting more diverse populations), cultivating more positive interracial interactions among college students, and enhancing students' perceptions of the campus racial climate in order to more effectively improve their campus racial climates for diversity. The climate framework also highlights the reality that structural diversity is only one of several factors influencing the climate of postsecondary campuses, but that institutional policies or practices and their behavioral and psychological effects are critical factors shaping the campus racial climate as well. This is an important point because scholars have argued that many college campuses focus on admitting more students of color, but fail to address the systemic racism that permeates their campuses (Chang, Chang, & Ledesma, 2005). The campus racial climate for diversity model highlights the reality that institutions must consider other factors that influence the climate if they seek to improve this aspect of their institutional environments.

One important limitation of the campus racial climate framework is that it does not delineate what an optimally inclusive, diverse, or equitable institution looks like. Therefore, higher education researchers, policy makers, and practitioners who engage the campus climate framework still might not have a clear vision for what they must do in order to make those institutions racially inclusive. The CECE Model, to which we now turn, is aimed at helping fill this gap.

The Culturally Engaging Campus Environments (CECE) Model

Although the terms *campus climate* and *campus culture* are sometimes used interchangeably, these two concepts are distinct (Bauer, 1998). Some authors have asserted that campus climate has to do with *current* perceptions, beliefs, and perspectives that exist within college campus environments, while the concept of campus culture refers to the *deeply embedded* cultural values, beliefs, attitudes, perspectives, and assumptions that permeate and shape behavior at postsecondary institutions. It has been argued that climate is more malleable, while culture is embedded within the institutional fabric of postsecondary campuses (Bauer, 1998). Thus, some scholars have argued that efforts to pursue long-term transformation of institutions to be more equitable must engage the concept of culture to be effective (Museus, Ravello, et al., 2012).

A substantial body of higher education literature illuminates the intersection between race and culture in shaping the experiences of students of color (Gonzalez, 2003; Kuh & Love, 2000; Museus, 2007, 2008, 2011; Museus & Harris, 2010; Museus & Quaye, 2009; Tierney, 1992, 1999). Indeed, White-dominant perspectives have informed the establishment and evolution of postsecondary campus cultures, and these cultures privilege the values, attitudes, assumptions, perspectives, and norms of the White dominant majority, while subordinating the cultural characteristics of minoritized communities (Museus, Ravello, et al., 2012). In doing so, these predominantly White institutional cultures often function as a pervasive mechanism of systemic racial oppression. As a result, people of color encounter unique and salient challenges as they transition and adjust to the cultures of their campuses that increase the likelihood that they will be unable to persist through the higher education system (Museus & Quaye, 2009).

The Culturally Engaging Campus Environments (CECE) Model of college success is based on the notion that institutions can construct campus cultures that meaningfully reflect and respond to the diverse backgrounds of their students in order to create the conditions for diverse student bodies to thrive (Museus, 2014, 2015). The model is designed to encourage postsecondary institutions to engage the cultural communities, backgrounds, and identities of diverse populations in the cultivation and enhancement of their curricula, programs, and practices. The CECE Model posits that external factors and precollege inputs influence students' college experiences. The focal point of the model, however, delineates the nine elements of campus environments that contribute to greater sense of belonging, higher levels of self-efficacy and motivation, greater satisfaction with the college experience, academic performance and learning, and persistence and completion. These nine elements of optimal campus environments are not mutually exclusive, but several of them can be integrated into specific spaces, curricula, programs, and or practices on college campuses. These nine elements include the following:

Cultural Relevance. Five indicators focus on the ways that campus learning environments are relevant to the cultural backgrounds, communities, and identities of diverse college students:

1. *Cultural familiarity:* The extent to which undergraduates have opportunities to connect with faculty, staff, and peers who share and understand their cultural backgrounds and experiences.

2. *Culturally relevant knowledge:* The degree to which students have opportunities to learn about their own cultural communities via culturally relevant curricular and cocurricular activities.
3. *Cultural community service:* Opportunities for students to give back to and positively transform their home communities (e.g., via problem-based research or service-learning).
4. *Meaningful cross-cultural engagement:* Programs and practices that facilitate educationally meaningful cross-cultural interactions that focus on solving real social and political problems.
5. *Culturally validating environments:* Campus cultures that validate the cultural backgrounds, knowledge, and identities of diverse students.

Cultural Responsiveness. The remaining four indicators focus on the ways in which campus learning and support systems engage and respond to the cultural norms and needs of diverse students:

1. *Collectivist cultural orientations:* Campus cultures that emphasize a collectivist, rather than individualistic, cultural orientation that is characterized by teamwork and pursuit of mutual success.
2. *Humanized educational environments:* Availability of opportunities to develop meaningful relationships with faculty and staff who care about and are committed to those students' success.
3. *Proactive philosophies:* Proactive philosophies that lead faculty, administrators, and staff to proactively bring important information, opportunities, and support services to students, rather than waiting for students to seek them out or hunt them down.
4. *Holistic support:* Students' access to at least one faculty or staff member that they are confident will provide the information they need, offer the help they seek, or connect them with the information or support they require regardless of the issue they face.

Like the other frameworks discussed above, the CECE Model makes important contributions to research and discourse around racism, how it manifests on college campuses, and how postsecondary institutions should strive to become more racially inclusive. Specifically, by outlining the types of environments that allow racially diverse populations to thrive, the CECE framework outlines a common evidence-based vision for institutions that seek to construct racially inclusive environments. The model is based on the assumption that racially inclusive environments are necessary to transform the cultures and structures of postsecondary institutions so that they reflect their diverse student bodies and allow racially diverse students to thrive.

Scholars have not yet generated a substantial body of literature to help understand how the framework applies to various institutional and individual processes, and such scholarship is needed. In addition, an important limitation of the CECE Model is that it does not provide insight into the different aspects of an institution that must be engaged or the process that campuses must learn to navigate in the pursuit of constructing culturally engaging campus environments. Several scholars have helped fill this gap in existing discourse around racism and racial equity in postsecondary education by offering useful frameworks for understanding institutions and change (e.g., Dowd & Bensimon, 2015; Kezar, 2012; Smith, 2011, 2015). We highlight two of these frameworks: the Institutional Diversity Framework and the Equity Scorecard.

The Institutional Diversity Framework
Smith (2011, 2015) has offered an institutional diversity framework that outlines aspects of the academic enterprise that need to be considered and engaged in holistic efforts to diversify college campuses. Her framework underscores the significance of global and local contexts within which postsecondary institutions exist. The framework for diversity also delineates five elements of college campuses that are critical to understanding diversity work in higher education. These five dimensions include the following:

1. *Mission:* The framework underscores the importance of aligning diversity with a mission of the institution.
2. *Institutional viability and vitality:* This dimension of the framework focuses on institutions' capacity and structures to promote diversity.
3. *Education and scholarship:* This dimension has to do with the extent to which diversity is integrated into the academic and educational domain of the institution.

4. *Climate and intergroup relations:* Aligned with the campus climate framework discussed above, this dimension focuses on the institutional climate and the extent to which campus community members interact with diverse groups.

5. *Access and success:* This dimension has to do with efforts to ensure opportunities for access and success to diverse populations.

One of the main contributions in the institutional diversity framework is that it outlines elements of the institution that need to be engaged if leaders seek to embed racial diversity, inclusion, and equity throughout their respective campuses. The framework underscores the reality that the campus climate is just one of several elements of broader institutional diversity.

Unfortunately, however, few higher education scholars have applied this framework to study organizational processes around institutional diversification. Again, such research might be useful in expanding our knowledge of how institutions can more holistically transform to be more racially equitable. One limitation of the institutional diversity framework is that it does not utilize existing literature to define what optimally inclusive environments should look like. However, it could be used in conjunction with the CECE Model to examine the extent to which college campuses have embedded indicators of culturally engaging environments throughout various aspects of their organizations. Another limitation of the institutional diversity framework is that it does not outline the elements of the *process* of pursuing an agenda that is aimed at achieving greater racial equity.

The Equity Scorecard

The Equity Scorecard is an action-research process framework that is designed to aid postsecondary institutions in understanding how to achieve more equitable outcomes (Bensimon & Malcolm, 2012; Dowd & Bensimon, 2015; Harris & Bensimon, 2007). Similar to other frameworks discussed herein, the Equity Scorecard aims to shed light on elements of postsecondary institutions that are often assumed to be objective but (dis)advantage certain racial groups. Similar to the CECE Model and the Institutional Diversity Framework, the Equity Scorecard emerged from the recognition of the importance of transcending a critical analysis of racism in higher education to better understand how to take action to achieve greater racial equity. However, the Equity Scorecard adds to previously discussed frameworks by outlining specific processes that can be engaged to achieve that effort. The process consists of the following components:

- *Data tools* that help institutions organize numerical data to understand key student outcomes (e.g., retention and degree completion) so that they are equipped to monitor progress toward racial equity.
- An *inquiry process* that guides institutions to transcend understanding inequities in student outcomes to constructing practices through which they can address those outcomes at their respective campuses.
- A *process of problem solving* that encourages team members to collaboratively develop an understanding of what contributes to inequities on their campuses.
- A *theory of change* that suggests that campuses must understand the ways in which their programs and practices are failing minoritized students.
- A *bottom-up approach to academic leadership* that emphasizes the power that faculty and staff, who are on the ground working with students, have to make change.
- A focus on developing *a culture of equity-mindedness* that promotes an awareness of racial inequities that permeate society and educational institutions, as well as the need to address them.

Unlike the models discussed above, the Equity Scorecard explicitly focuses on the process of practitioner inquiry as the catalyst for change. In doing so, it acknowledges the complexity of organizational dynamics and transformation in racial equity agendas at postsecondary institutions. One limitation of the Equity Scorecard is that it arguably does not sufficiently and explicitly engage the decades of existing research and knowledge regarding the types of institutions that maximize racial equity and thriving among minoritized populations. Similarly, it does not explicitly outline the elements of higher education institutions that must be included in efforts to achieve greater racial equity.

Conclusion

In sum, several racially conscious frameworks have been applied to the study of postsecondary systems and experiences within them. They constitute conceptual lenses to understand how racism operates within systems of higher education and how higher education scholars, policy makers, and practitioners can address this systemic problem. The ways in which racism operates the foci of the next two chapters of the current volume to which we now turn.

Historical and Contemporary Racial Contexts

I N THIS CHAPTER, we discuss critical historical and contemporary racial context. First, we review key historical trends and events that provide important context for understanding how racism shapes the experiences of people in U.S. society. In doing so, we provide an overview of key racial processes that aid in understanding how racism has operated and evolved within U.S. social systems. Then, we discuss how racism operates in society in the present day, focusing on contemporary forms of racism and color-blind ideologies that permeate the United States.

Historical Foundations of Racism in Society

Racism is often discussed in ahistorical ways. Failing to acknowledge the historical roots and evolution of racism in society contributes to misunderstandings and false notions that racial progress has been steady and deliberate. Racism permeates U.S. history, and this historical context is critical to understanding how racism operates in the present day (Feagin, 2006; Lowen, 1996; Zinn, 2005). Therefore, in this section, we discuss some of the critical historical context that contributes to the nature of contemporary racism in higher education. It is important to note that a thorough analysis of the racial history of the United States is beyond the scope of this volume. Therefore, we do not claim that this discussion is comprehensive. Nor do we claim that this historical overview illuminates the historical context of the United

States with sufficient depth and complexity. Rather, we choose to provide a brief summary of some key historical trends and events that are critical to understanding racism in higher education today.

In the scholarly arena, it is now fairly widely accepted that race is not a biological phenomenon, but is instead a social construct (Gould, 1996; Haney López, 1996; Omi & Winant, 2015). To comprehend how race is socially constructed, it is useful to understand the concepts of racial formation and racialization. The term *racial formation* signifies the process by which economic, political, and social forces shape racial categories, the meanings that get attached to those categories, and their importance (Omi & Winant, 1994). The concept of racial formation also suggests that, because race and racial categories are not natural but are socially constructed phenomena, these categories and their corresponding meanings vary across space and time. And, as we illuminate in this section, processes of racial formation have manifested in the evolution of race and racism since European settlers made contact with the United States.

Within racial systems, subordinated racial groups are racialized. The term *racialization* refers to the process of constructing racial categories, attaching these racial labels to previously unclassified groups or social practices, and attaching race-based meanings to these categories and their corresponding populations (Omi & Winant, 1994). *Differential racialization* denotes the reality that different groups are racialized in unique ways. These concepts are useful in helping us understand how race and racism have operated throughout history and, as we discuss herein, racism has led to different minoritized populations being racialized in distinct ways that subordinate them and preserve power and privilege for the dominant majority.

It is important to understand the origins of race and racism in Western society. Hundreds of years ago, race and racism emerged as a significant element of the social order when European explorers made contact with non-European communities (Omi & Winant, 1994). These explorers found people around the globe with physical characteristics and cultures that deviated from their own, and they constructed a race-based worldview to help them make sense of these differences. In the process, these explorers racially categorized foreign populations as different and inferior to their own communities.

Europeans utilized this racialization of populations as inferior beings to justify their racial oppression of various communities of color around the world (Omi & Winant, 1994). Indeed, the conclusion that groups of people around the globe were inferior to those from the Western world provided a race-based justification of denying those communities equal rights, coercing them into certain forms of labor, subjecting them to slavery, and even exterminating them and their cultures.

Not long after Christopher Columbus and other European settlers first entered the United States in the late 1400s, tensions emerged. European colonists began stripping Native Americans of their lands (Lomawaima & McCarty, 2006; Prucha, 1995; Tinker, 1993). The acquisition of land from Native communities led to conflict, which ultimately resulted in the massacre and mass genocide of Native populations across the United States, as well as efforts to eradicate their culture and utilize education to force them to assimilate into European American society.

In the early 1600s, the first Black slaves were captured and brought from Africa to the United States (Feagin, 2006). Prior to the mid-1800s, many Black people in the United States were considered the property of White slave owners and had few rights. And, while some might consider slavery far removed from the present day, the history of slavery is critical to understanding the current conditions of many Black communities in the United States. It is important to note that the Black slaves were brought to the United States as free labor to fuel the economic interests of White colonists (Feagin, 2006).

Although some people from Asia began to immigrate into the United States in the 1700s, they began entering the nation in large numbers in the mid-1800s (Chan, 1991; Takaki, 1989; Zia, 2001). Because of a shortage of Black slaves, many Chinese were brought to the continental United States to fill the void. In addition, some Chinese prospected for gold but were forced to pay an ethnic "tax" on Chinese miners. If the Chinese protested the tax, they were beaten or murdered. Other Chinese immigrants worked on the transcontinental railroads and were forced to labor under life-threatening conditions that led to them dying by dynamite explosion in larger numbers. In addition, the Chinese railroad workers were often viewed as more efficient than White workers, and were therefore brought to the United States in large numbers to complete the railroads. As a result, a backlash by White workers ensued, resulting in the lynching and mass murder of many Chinese immigrants. Asians who immigrated to Hawaii as contract-laborers were also subject to inhumane conditions on plantations, which some argued were equivalent to the conditions in which many Black slaves lived on the continental United States (Takaki, 1989).

The ways in which racism shapes Mexican American experiences also have important historical roots (Acuña, 2014; Feagin & Cobas, 2014; Valencia, 2008). In the mid-1800s, manifest destiny, disputes over territory in the Southwest, the U.S. annexation of Texas, and the resulting Mexican-American War fueled anti-Mexican sentiment in the states (Brack, 1970). In addition, just as the lynching of Chinese immigrants is often overlooked in American history, the lynching of Mexican and Mexican Americans is rarely discussed in history books (Delgado, 2009). This exclusion of Chinese and Mexican Americans from U.S. history could partially be due to the fact that, at the time, victims of lynching incidents were racially classified as Black or White, and Chinese and Mexican victims were recorded as White. Nevertheless, some scholars have estimated that approximately 600 Mexicans and Mexican Americans were lynched between 1848 and 1928 alone (Carrigan & Web, 2003; Delgado, 2009). And, from the Great Depression of the 1930s to today, Mexican American communities have been targeted in immigrant raids and deported to Mexico in large numbers (Hoffman, 1974).

The end of the Civil War in 1865 brought new hope and the promise of freedom and opportunity for Blacks and other people of color in the United States. However, after the mid-19th century, racism proved to be resistant to change by assuming a different face and form. Although it was no longer legal for White people to own Black slaves and other people of color, overt systemic and individual racism evolved and persisted throughout society in new ways (Feagin, 2006). For example, White backlash occurred after the Civil War during reconstruction (Wood, 1968), and included the emergence of the influential White supremacist organization called the Ku Klux Klan. People of color were still treated as inferior, forced to use different facilities than their White counterparts, and were denied access to social institutions, including K–12 schools and institutions of higher education (Feagin, 2006).

In addition, xenophobia led to policies that prevented Asian immigrants from entering the United States, such as the Chinese Exclusion Act of 1882 and Gentleman's Agreement Act of 1907 with Japan (Chan, 1991; Takaki, 1989; Tamura, 2001a, 2001b; Museus, 2013b).

Westerners made contact with Hawaii in the late 1700s, and introduced diseases that killed the vast majority of the Native Hawaiian population (Kame'eleihiwa, 1992). On the Hawaiian Islands in 1893, a group of American businessmen decided to illegally overthrow the Hawaiian monarchy (Trask, 2000). As the sugar industry in Hawaii became increasingly lucrative, American businessmen seized increased control of affairs in Hawaii and, with backing of American troops, staged a coup. As a result, Hawaiian Queen Lili'uokalani relinquished her throne, under protest, to avoid bloodshed. And, since her overthrow, education has been utilized as a tool in the colonization of the Hawaiian islands and marginalization of Hawaiian culture with Westernized education systems.

In the late 1700s, under the notion of expansionism, Western explorers also spread their influence into other parts of the Pacific Ocean (Blaut, 1993). Motivated by scientific and economic interests, voyagers made contact with regions of the Pacific and exposed them to the rest of the globe. Over time, Western interests in the Pacific shifted to be economic and military in nature (Robie, 1990). As a result, the United States and other Western nations colonized islands of the Pacific for economic and military purposes, and U.S. colonization and militarization of the Pacific have had permanent effects on the Pacific Islands and its peoples. The United States used the Pacific Islands as locations to house military bases and as a space to test military weapons (e.g., torpedoes, bombs, nuclear arms, etc.). For example, between 1946 and 1958, the United States tested a total of 66 atomic and hydrogen bombs in the Marshall Islands, leaving many islands uninhabitable because of high levels of radiation and long-lasting health problems among Pacific Islander communities due to exposure from such radiation. Consequently, the federal government has opened its doors to some victims of this U.S. military activity, and many Pacific Islanders have migrated to the United States to access cancer and other medical treatments. These are just some of the ways in which the racial subjugation and exploitation of communities in the Pacific Islands have shaped the lives of Pacific Islanders in the United States and their trajectories to and through its education system.

Racial victories of the Civil Rights Movement in the mid-20th century catalyzed another shift in the way racism operated in the United States. The Civil Rights Movement and key events that occurred as part of that effort rendered explicit racism less socially acceptable. For example, the Supreme Court's decision in *Brown v. Board of Education* (1954) declared that "separate" could no longer be considered "equal" and eventually put an end to formal de jure segregation in the United States (Bell, 1980). In addition, the Civil Rights Act of 1964 outlawed discrimination on the basis of race and sex in hiring, promoting, and firing practices. After these landmark decisions began to inch toward providing people of color with equal protection of the law, racism again adapted to operate effectively despite these advances. Specifically, because the majority could no longer legally discriminate against people of color on the basis of race, more covert forms of racism emerged. For example, scholars have documented the ways in which the passage of the Civil Rights Act was followed by a backlash, including the persecution of Black radical intellectuals and housing discrimination that channeled people of color into segregated communities, thereby maintaining the de facto racial segregation of communities and K–12 schools, as well as solidifying inequities within the education system (Delgado Bernal, 2002; Selmi, 1997).

This analysis generates at least three critical themes that permeate the history of racism in the United States and provides important context for the current volume. First, the racial history of the nation is one of both progress *and* regress. As progressive advocates have advanced racial equity agendas in the United States, those accomplishments have been met with and followed by racial backlash and an evolution of racism that allowed it to function effectively under new legal and social conditions. Second, these events demonstrate that the history of various communities of color in the United States, while sharing common experiences of racial oppression and economic exploitation, is unique. Indeed, the process of differential racialization has led to distinct histories, conditions, and experiences across groups of color (Delgado & Stefancic, 2001). Finally, these historical events demonstrate that racism and economic exploitation are inextricably intertwined, as they reveal how the racial domination and subordination of communities of color have always been pursued in the economic interest of the majority. Central to this volume is the reality that racism, education, and economic exploitation are all arguably interconnected. As postsecondary education has become increasingly essential to succeeding economically, the aforementioned de facto racial segregation has functioned to ensure that people of color are disproportionately channeled into trajectories that result in less educational, and consequently economic, opportunities and prosperity. In recent years, there has been increased attention given to new forms of racism that emerged after the Civil Rights era and the color-blind ideologies that mask them. In the next section, we discuss these two phenomena, which largely characterize the racial challenges of U.S. society in the 21st century.

From Old to New Forms of Racism in Society

Over the past half-century, racism and the way it operates have evolved. Since the Civil Rights Movement of the 1960s, there has been a growing perception that racism is no longer a problem in the United States (Bonilla-Silva, 2003). For example, members of the White majority across the United States frequently point to isolated racial victories, such as the aforementioned election of a Black President, as compelling evidence that racism no longer exists or at least is not a major factor in determining access to opportunity (Bonilla-Silva, 2003). Unfortunately, however, these claims of a post-racial society ignore the reality that our nation has evolved from a history of racial oppression and that the weight of evidence suggests that systemic racism still permeates social institutions and daily life.

New forms of racial oppression that emerged in the latter half of the 20th century are much more difficult to detect than past forms of racism (Bonilla-Silva, 2003; Sue, 2003). Today, the law prohibits racial discrimination and racially motivated hate crimes against people of color. People of color are no longer forced to utilize different and subpar resources compared to their White counterparts, and now legally have access to the same facilities and educational institutions as the majority. Nevertheless, racism continues to plague the nation (Sue, 2003).

Whereas "old fashioned" racism manifested in overt expressions of White racial superiority, racism has evolved into more ambiguous, subtle, and subconscious manifestations (Dovidio, Gaertner, Kawakami, & Hodson, 2002; Sue, 2003). Researchers have argued that this new racism is more likely to be evident in the thinking and behaviors of well-intentioned Whites who hold beliefs and engage in behaviors that seem benign on the surface but are nevertheless detrimental to people of color (Banaji, 2001; DeVos & Banaji, 2005). Thus, it has been said that these new forms of racism are invisible (Tinsley-Jones, 2003), or operate in a *now you see it, now you don't* fashion (Bonilla-Silva, 2003). To label this new racism, researchers have coined terms such as "subtle racism," "symbolic racism," and "aversive racism" to describe how new forms of racism manifest in covert or subtle ways in an era where explicit racism is increasingly socially unacceptable (Sears, 1988; Sue, Bucceri, et al., 2007). Similarly, scholars have begun to utilize the concept of "racial microaggressions" to refer to manifestations of this new racism. Racial microaggressions have been defined as, "brief and commonplace daily verbal, behavioral, or environmental indignities, whether intentional or unintentional, that communicate hostile, derogatory, or negative racial slights and insults toward people of color" (Sue, Capodilupo, et al., 2007, p. 271). For example, a common racial microaggression targeted toward Black people is behavior that sends them a message that they do not belong (e.g., store clerks who are reluctant to interact with Black persons) (Sue, Capodilupo, & Holder, 2008), while a common microaggression aimed at Asian Americans is the denial of their racial realities (e.g., "Asians are the new Whites") leading to the misconception that they do not face race-related challenges (Sue, Bucceri, et al., 2007, p. 76).

To understand how these new forms of racism operate, it is important to consider the emergence of dominant color-blind ideologies, which can mask the salience of racism in society. Today, relatively few people would admit that they are racist (Bonilla-Silva, 2003). And, *color-blind racism* refers to the reality that most Whites in the United States claim to be color-blind, aspire to live in a society where people are not judged by the color of their skin, and claim that racism does not influence them or their views of other people. Many argue that any racism that needs to be eradicated has already been eliminated and, when we focus on racism, we pay too much attention to a problem that no longer exists. A majority of White people also believe that people of color are responsible for whatever race-related problems linger in the United States and, when racism and its effects are invoked in daily conversation, people often blame persons of color for having a self-defeating mentality and "playing the race card." The sentiment is that, if Black and Brown people would just stop feeling sorry for themselves and work harder, then the nation's race-related problems would disappear.

Although older forms of racism were based on the belief that people of color were biologically or genetically inferior, new forms of racism highlight cultural deficiencies among communities of color as a primary factor leading to racial inequalities in society (Bonilla-Silva, 2003). For example, widely read authors have made the claim that the struggles of Black people are not a function of systemic racism, but are instead a consequence of cultural inadequacies within the Black community (Brooks, 2015). This cultural deficit–based perspective places primary burden of responsibility for persisting racial inequalities on the shoulders of people of color while downplaying systemic racism in society. And, these deficit perspectives permeate contemporary color-blind perspectives held toward communities of color in the United States.

Indeed, critics of race-consciousness have chosen to champion color-blindness. Haney López (2014) observes that the prevailing etiquette around race is color-blindness. He explains,

> [Color-blindness] has a strong moral appeal, for it laudably envisions an ideal world in which race is no longer relevant to how we perceive and treat each other. It also has an intuitive practical appeal: to get beyond race, color blindness urges, the best strategy is to immediately stop recognizing and talking about race. (pp. 77–78)

Omi and Winant (2015) echo this concern, positing that color blindness has come to represent a new kind of racial hegemony. The emergence of color blindness as a new form of racial domination constitutes an urgent need for discourse that deconstructs the notion of race neutrality, (re)centers the permanence of racism in social institutions, and unpacks how racism continues to shape and frame higher educational opportunities for people of color.

In *Racism Without Racists*, Bonilla-Silva (2003) outlines the four dominant frames that contribute to and characterize color-blind perspectives in the United States in the present day. These frames of color blindness delineated by Bonilla-Silva (2003) depict the ways in which people make sense of the role of race in American society, causes of racial inequalities, and the experiences of people of color. The first frame, *abstract liberalism*, is the utilization of ideas associated with political liberalism (e.g., equal opportunity) and economic liberalism (e.g., freedom of choice and individualism) in abstract ways to explain racial phenomena. Second, *naturalization* refers to the ways in which Whites explain away racial realities as natural occurrences. Third, *cultural racism* refers to the idea that racial phenomena are a result of cultural differences, such as "Black people do not care about education," to explain inequalities in society. And, finally, *minimization of racism* suggests that while racial discrimination may continue to exist, it does not persist in ways that are significant enough to affect the life chances and outcomes of different racial groups. Bonilla-Silva argues that people use these color-blind frames to absolve themselves from any responsibility for racial inequalities. And, several critical race theorists have also underscored this phenomenon in their work (Delgado & Stefancic, 2001; Ladson-Billings & Tate, 1995; Matsuda et al., 1993). These color-blind frames are essential to developing an understanding of the ways in which color blindness shapes people's understanding of racism today, manifests in everyday behavior and language, diminishes the significance of racism in contemporary society, and is used to discount notions of persisting racial oppression.

It is also important to recognize that other dominant systemic forces are inextricably intertwined with racism and how it operates. One of these major social forces is *neoliberalism*, a trend that increasingly influences the lives of people throughout society and emphasizes support for greater economic liberalization, free trade and market deregulation, decreased public spending, and increased privatization (Giroux, 2010; Kellner, 2000). Scholars have written that this neoliberalization of society has generated a climate in which individual freedom and the exchange of capital take precedence over all other domains of American life, such as social justice, long-standing social contracts, the education and preparation of socially conscious and responsible citizens, and the building and maintenance of democratic communities. Thus, neoliberal ideologies intersect with racism, and promote and perpetuate ways of thinking that highlight individual responsibility in creating racial and other social conditions, while reinforcing color-blind ideologies and downplaying the role of racism in bringing about such conditions.

Conclusion

Understanding the historical and contemporary nature of racism is critical for higher education scholars, policy makers, and practitioners to comprehend the complexity of the ways in which racism permeates postsecondary institutions, as well as how they might engage in efforts to address them. These racial realities underscore the deep roots and persistent nature of racism in the fabric of the United States and therefore in its higher education system. If racism is so deeply ingrained throughout society and social institutions, policies and practices that work to address symptoms of racism in higher education without challenging the institutional systems that facilitate such racism are superficial at best. More profound change requires challenging dominant core values, beliefs, assumptions, policies, and practices that perpetuate and propagate White supremacist and color-blind ideologies.

Systemic Racism in
Higher Education

I N THIS CHAPTER, we discuss the ways in which systemic racism shapes
higher education systems and experiences within them. Specifically, we discuss how racism has influenced the development and execution of some of the
most influential policies in higher education history. Then, we analyze high-
profile contemporary policy issues in higher education from a race-conscious
lens. In doing so, we highlight how racism and color-blind ideologies are shaping current policy discourse in postsecondary education. Next, we examine
how racism shapes the experiences of faculty within institutions of higher education. Finally, we provide an overview of research on how racism shapes the
lives of students of color in college.

Manifestations of Racism in
Higher Education History

As mentioned in the Introduction, higher education was originally designed
to serve the White majority, and prepare White men for leadership roles in
society (Karabel, 2005; Thelin, 2011). Since this genesis, racism has manifested in higher education policy at federal, state, and institutional levels.
For example, the establishment of Historically Black Colleges and Universities (HBCUs) and Tribal Colleges and Universities (TCUs) during the 19th
century exemplifies how racism has informed seemingly objective and progressive higher education policy. These Minority Serving Institutions (MSIs)

have served large numbers of college students of color, and it could easily be assumed that their establishment was benign or altruistic. However, scholars have argued that the establishment of these campuses reflects Whites' historical unwillingness to accommodate students of color within their own higher education systems, but readiness to help establish separate institutions for students of color that maintained a racially segregated postsecondary education system. Indeed, intentions of the founders of MSIs were sometimes characterized by racism (Gasman, 2008).

In this section, we offer examples of how racism provides important context for understanding higher education policy and responses to it in history. Specifically, we present an overview of what are arguably three of the most racially progressive policies of 20th-century higher education: (1) the Morrill Land Grant Acts, (2) the Servicemen's Readjustment Act or the G.I. Bill, and (3) affirmative action. These examples demonstrate how even the most well-intentioned policies that have been aimed at ensuring access to opportunity for all people can function to reinforce racial inequities, prompt society to reconfigure systems to ensure that such policies do not help achieve equity, or face constant challenges from the dominant majority.

The Morrill Land Grant Acts of 1862 and 1890 allocated federal land and funding for states to establish and for the expansion of preexisting and new public colleges and universities (Thelin, 2011). The 1862 Morrill Act provided federal funding for the establishment of land grant colleges in each state. Several states, however, had segregated systems and excluded students from their land grant colleges. Thus, Congress passed the second Morrill Act of 1890, which provided funding for these states to establish separate land grant colleges for Black students. Through this mass expansion, the Morrill Land Grant Acts helped make higher education more accessible to students of color who were previously denied access to learning opportunities at the nation's predominantly White colleges and universities. However, while the Morrill Acts widened the gates of opportunity for historically disenfranchised communities, the policy also helped sustain and promote racial inequality (Harper, Patton, & Wooden, 2009). For example, the 1890 Act's establishment of Black state-supported institutions facilitated the segregation of Black and White public postsecondary campuses and promoted a curricular emphasis on mechanics, agriculture, and industrial fields among Blacks. And, it has been argued that this model legalized the inequitable segregation of public colleges and universities and promoted the notion that Black students were inferior to Whites and deserved a distinct and lower-quality education (Harper et al., 2009). It is important to note that, in the absence of a critical and historical contextual analysis, these realities are minimized or completely dismissed.

The G.I. Bill provides another example of how higher education policy that expands opportunity for all students on the surface can prompt responses that reinscribe racial oppression and inequities. Indeed, the G.I. Bill has long been touted as one of the principal democratizing policies of the past century (Brubacher & Rudy, 1997). The G.I. Bill did prove to be monumental in expanding higher education through booming enrollments that sparked massive construction of laboratories, buildings, and dormitories (Thelin, 2011). At the same time, however, analyzing the bill from a racially conscious lens suggests that it further reified racism and racial inequities throughout higher education (Katznelson, 2005). While the G.I. Bill was intended to grant educational benefits to *all* eligible returning World War II servicemen, it proved to be less than equitable in practice. Whereas White veterans were much more likely to cash in their full benefits, veterans of color were often denied access to their subsidies. Even when veterans of color were successful in accessing their G.I. Bill benefits, they were frequently tracked into vocational programs and less-selective colleges and universities (Katznelson, 2005; Thelin, 2011). Therefore these minoritized veterans' lack of access to quality institutions undermined the positive aims of the bill (Katznelson, 2005). And, the promises of the G.I. Bill were largely illusory and intangible for a disproportionate number of veterans of color.

Among the most controversial policies in the quest for racial equity in higher education has been the use of race in admissions decisions. Affirmative action was introduced during the latter half of the 20th century. Originating with President John F. Kennedy's Executive Order 10925, affirmative action sought to facilitate an end to racial discrimination in federal contracting (Skrentny, 1996). While President Kennedy's original order was largely intended to address the business sector, the application of affirmative action in higher education was ushered in under President Lyndon Johnson's administration. Within the realm of higher education, affirmative action was aimed at facilitating racial integration within the nation's most selective public and private colleges and universities. Several Supreme Court cases, which we discuss in the following sections, have affirmed postsecondary institutions' right to the limited use of race in admissions processes. Race-conscious practices enable these campuses to admit larger numbers of historically underrepresented students into their institutions by using more than test scores, which evidence indicates are racially biased and disadvantage these populations in admissions processes (Jencks & Phillips, 2011).

In sum, racism has played a prominent role in higher education history. And, these historical realities provide an important background for our discussion of contemporary manifestations of racism in postsecondary education systems, to which we now turn.

Racism in Higher Education Policy

Although the ways in which racism affects contemporary higher education policy are subtler than in the past, postsecondary education policy continues to be intimately shaped by it. For example, it has been argued that the rationales that typically drive policy making are designed by the elite to shape higher education policy in ways that benefit the elite (St. John, Daun-Barnett, & Moronski-Chapman, 2013). Given that the "elite" class in the United States is disproportionately composed of members of the White majority, it could be argued that the power elite's policy rationales can and do function to preserve power, status, and opportunity for the disproportionately White elite while limiting access to these privileges among historically marginalized and minoritized populations.

In this section, we explore some of the ways in which racism might manifest in higher education policy. Specifically, we discuss some of the ways in which racism might shape policy decisions and processes in the areas of standardized testing, affirmative action, higher education finance, and other emerging policy issues. In doing so, we demonstrate how critical analysis of each of these policy issues can begin to illuminate how racism in higher education policy making continues to limit educational access and opportunity for students from minoritized populations.

Racism and Standardized Testing

Long before students enter higher education, racism begins to shape their educational trajectories. For example, racism influences precollege educational trajectories and college opportunities through channeling minoritized students into underresourced schools, tracking students of color into remedial and vocational pathways, providing these students with limited access to college preparatory honors and advanced placement coursework, and denying these students access to quality college counseling and advising services (Oakes, 2005; Oakes, Rogers, Lipton, & Morrell, 2002; Solórzano & Ornelas, 2002, 2004). And, the imposition of inequitable admissions requirements, such as standardized test scores, exacerbates these already existing inequities.

It is important to note that standardized aptitude tests have roots in the eugenics movement (Bond, 1924; Gould, 1996; Karabel, 2005). Eugenics was founded on the belief that it is possible to distinguish between superior and inferior races, and the notion that historically oppressed racial groups are inherently less intelligent than their majoritarian White counterparts. Eugenics also served as a foundational pillar for the production of intelligence tests, which were utilized to sort racial groups, rank their intelligence, and exclude people of color from full participation in society and education.

Indeed, intelligence tests have long been used to justify the perpetuation of racism (Gould, 1996; Karabel, 2005). For example, before the Civil War, slave owners used these tests to rationalize their inhumane treatment of people of color as the appropriate way to deal with populations that they considered intellectually inferior. Likewise, early army intelligence tests were utilized to classify "Negroes, Mexicans, and Indians" as drawn from "inferior homes" and exhibiting "racial dullness" (Bond, 1924, p. 594). Similarly, the institutionalization of standardized tests within the education system, such as the SAT, was originally meant to distinguish the aristocracy from the working class (Karabel, 2005; Lemann, 2000). Thus, standardized aptitude tests were historically designed and utilized as a tool of exclusion.

Standardized tests fuel misconceptions that exam scores offer an objective measure of academic ability and that education is a meritocratic system. Unfortunately, studies have exposed how test scores are not necessarily objective measures of intelligence (Au, 2009). Atkinson and Geiser (2009) explain how family income and parents' educational background are largely responsible for the apparent power of standardized tests in predicting students' first-year success in college. In other words, standardized test scores primarily serve as a proxy for socioeconomic status, and aptitude tests function as a mechanism to promote the institutions' selection and admission of applicants from more affluent backgrounds and with college-educated parents.

In addition, the concept of stereotype threat calls into the question the predictive validity of standardized tests (Steele & Aronson, 1995). Stereotype threat refers to the ways in which racial stereotypes can pose an environmental threat that has harmful effects on test performance. Specifically, scholars have demonstrated that where racial stereotypes that depict students of color as intellectually inferior exist in the environment, they can create anxiety and result in lower performance among students of color who belong to the communities targeted by those stereotypes (Steele, 1999; Steele & Aronson, 1995). Therefore, a legacy of White supremacy and racism can have a significant negative impact on the standardized test performance of students of color, resulting in fewer educational opportunities.

In sum, standardized tests perpetuate false notions of meritocracy and mask existing systemic inequities in educational opportunity. They are mainly a proxy for socioeconomic status, rather than a unique measure of academic ability. And, coupled with stereotypes that some students of color cannot perform as well as their peers on these exams, standardized tests can function to further disadvantage minoritized populations in the admissions process. While a growing number of institutions are choosing to opt out of requiring standardized test scores from prospective applicants (Bidwell, 2015), the majority of colleges and universities still do require such scores for admission and consider them in admissions decisions.

Racism and Affirmative Action Debates

In 1978, in *Regents of the University of California v. Bakke*, the Supreme Court ruled that race-conscious admissions policies were constitutional. In the majority opinion resulting from *Bakke*, the Court concluded that diversity was a compelling state interest. The opinion noted that race-conscious admissions were necessary to enable institutions of higher education to construct environments characterized by diverse student bodies, which contribute to conditions that reduce students' prejudice and facilitate their learning through the exposure to different viewpoints. Since the *Bakke* ruling, many proponents of affirmative action have primarily relied on the diversity rationale to defend race-conscious policies because of their utility in producing racially diverse student bodies so that students have opportunities to interact across difference.

Since the *Bakke* (1978) decision, the issue of affirmative action in university admissions has been heard before the Supreme Court in three more cases. In the University of Michigan's 2003 affirmative action cases, *Gratz v. Bollinger* (2003) and *Grutter v. Bollinger* (2003), the Court struck down Michigan's race-conscious undergraduate admissions plan in *Gratz* while upholding the legality of the Law School's race-conscious admissions practices in *Grutter.* Ten years later, in *Fisher v. University of Texas at Austin* (2013), the Court once again ruled in favor of the university's limited use of race in university admissions practices. In these decisions, the Court reinforced the legality of race-conscious admissions, but asserted that there must be a compelling interest and race-conscious policies must be narrowly tailored to achieve that interest. In addition, central to the Supreme Court's decisions in *Grutter* and *Fisher* were arguments emphasizing the importance of a "critical mass" for underrepresented students. The critical mass rationale is based on evidence suggesting that students are more likely to succeed when they are surrounded by a critical mass (i.e., significant numbers) of peers who share their backgrounds (Museus, Jayakumar, & Robinson, 2012). The argument suggests that, in the absence of a critical mass, minoritized students are more likely to experience racial isolation and tokenism, causing them to be at greater risk of stopping or dropping out. On the other hand, if students of color are able to foster connections with substantial numbers of institutional agents who share their backgrounds, they are more likely to succeed (Museus, 2014). Critics of affirmative action object to the critical mass argument by framing it as nothing more than a veiled smokescreen for illegal quotas.

It is important to note that the diversity rationale sometimes deemphasizes the reality that affirmative action is aimed at combatting continuing systemic racism (Jayakumar & Adamian, 2015). In the short term, legal strategy to focus on the diversity rationale and deemphasize antiracism as the primary defense for affirmative action has allowed race-conscious policies to survive legal scrutiny. However, in the long run, the absence of systemic racism from affirmative action discourse might make race-conscious policies more susceptible to critique. For instance, in the absence of a focus on reaffirming the role of affirmative action in combatting systemic racism, critics of race-conscious admissions policies have engaged ideological narratives that promote color blindness and post-racialism to dismiss the role of racism in shaping college opportunity and contend that policies like affirmative action are no longer necessary. These critics have also been able to argue that affirmative action perpetrates and perpetuates reverse racism because it disadvantages Whites who, they inaccurately suggest, are on a level playing field with people of color. And, opponents of affirmative action have underscored the "mismatch" hypothesis, or the view that supposed beneficiaries of race-conscious policies are actually ill served because they are often admitted to postsecondary institutions for which they are academically unprepared (Sander & Taylor, 2012; Thernstrom & Thernstrom, 1997). Of course, the evidence of persisting systemic racism reveals flaws in these arguments, as it (a) debunks myths that racism no longer shapes individual life chances and (b) exposes the mismatch argument as fundamentally racist because it suggests that students of color are academically ill equipped to succeed in the nation's most competitive postsecondary institutions.

Although the diversity rationale has been the primary defense for race-conscious policies over the past 30 years, one underlying purpose of affirmative action has always been to combat systemic racism. Indeed, when President John F. Kennedy issued Executive Order 10925 in 1961, it included a provision that government contractors should take affirmative action to minimize the likelihood that employees face discrimination based on race, creed, color, or national origin. Therefore, at its origins, affirmative action was a mechanism to minimize the effects of racism and other forms of social oppression affecting marginalized populations. And, members of the Supreme Court have recently reasserted that race continues to matter in determining people's life chances (*Schuette v. Coalition to Defend affirmative action*, 2014).

Opponents of race-conscious policies are unrelenting in their efforts to overturn the legality of affirmative action in higher education and beyond. With the Supreme Court's recent decision to rehear *Fisher v. University of Texas at Austin*, they will have another opportunity to do so. The evidence that racism still plays a prominent role in shaping the experiences and outcomes of people in society, coupled with the emergent understanding that critical mass on college campuses might be necessary to provide vital support to minoritized students who still have to navigate racist educational systems, might offer a more holistic understanding of the necessity of affirmative action policies and more comprehensive defensible argument for the continuation of race-conscious admissions practices in postsecondary education.

Racism and Higher Education Finance

Many challenges to college affordability persist. As we discuss in this section, state divestment from higher education, rising college costs, an increased reliance on loans, and for-profit colleges and predatory practices all create additional barriers to college affordability for low-income students. And, although not all students of color come from financially disadvantaged backgrounds, they are more likely to originate from economically underresourced communities (see the first chapter, "Introduction"). Thus, it could be hypothesized that the aforementioned processes that limit the affordability of postsecondary education work to disproportionately limit the capacity of students of color to pay for a college education.

While there was once a general consensus that government had a role to play in promoting social and economic progress, conservative politicians have recast social programs as too costly to justify taxpayer support over the past half-century (St. John et al., 2013). In part as a result in this recasting, over the past 25 years, state support for higher education has waned (Oliff, Palacios, Johnson, & Leachman, 2013; The Pew Charitable Trusts, 2015). The state divestment from financing postsecondary education has also arguably been precipitated by a shift in the perceived primary purpose of postsecondary education from a facilitator of a democratic society to a mechanism of social mobility, and shift in the view from higher education serving as a public good to a private good (Labaree, 1997).

At the same time that state governments have divested from the funding of higher education institutions, average college tuition prices have continued to rise, placing an increased burden of financing higher education on students and their families (College Board, 2014). Moreover, over the past few decades, the composition of financial aid packages for college students has shifted from an emphasis on need-based grants to an increasing reliance on merit-based aid and loans. It has been argued that this shift has had a disproportionately negative impact on already disadvantaged students in higher education (e.g., low-income students and students of color) (Long & Riley, 2007). One reason that the increased reliance on loans in the composition of financial aid packages might disproportionately negatively affect the trajectories of low-income students and students of color is that they are more loan-averse than their White and more affluent peers, making it less likely for them to take advantage of the benefits of heavily loan-dependent financial aid packages. Thus, the rise in tuition coupled with an increased reliance on loans in the composition of financial aid packages and high levels of debt aversion among college students of color can serve to limit their access to higher education opportunities (Heller, 2006). This is just one example of how recent trends in higher education finance have systemically served to limit opportunities among low-income students and students of color.

Although there have been some efforts to relieve the financial burden of paying for college among students, close examination of these efforts reveals how they have limited impact on low-income students and students of color. For example, some elite institutions have adopted no-loan programs to ensure that low-income students can afford the education they provide. These no-loan programs have proven to have a positive effect on enrolling and retaining low-income students (Hillman, 2013). However, elite institutions are much more likely to be able to sponsor no-loan programs, and these institutions enroll only a small portion of students in higher education. As such, large numbers of low-income students continue to rely heavily on federal financial aid to pay for college.

Another example of efforts to relieve low-income families of the financial burden of paying for college has been moderate increases in federal Pell

Grants. While Pell Grants have proven to be especially effective in helping low-income students subsidize their education, state governments have responded to moderate increases in these awards by decreasing their own financial support of higher education, thereby forcing state institutions to increase tuition and fees and "nullifying" federal efforts to increase aid and lower costs for financially needy students (Bok, 2013, p. 101). Thus, even as a college education becomes more and more indispensable, the affordability of quality educational opportunities continues to be inequitable, especially for low-income students and students of color.

Racism and Emerging Policy Issues

Racism can also be used to engage in the critical analysis of two emerging policy issues: performance funding and for-profit higher education. Indeed, one of the most pressing issues throughout U.S. higher education is the urgency of improving college persistence and graduation rates (Jones, 2014). As a result, many states are adopting performance funding models, in which institutional performance is evaluated using metrics that typically revolve around retention and graduation rates. In fact, over half of the states have adopted or are in the process of adopting performance-based systems (Friedel, Thornton, D'Amico, & Kantsinas, 2013).

While some performance funding models have equity measures, these policies have been critiqued for many reasons (Jones, 2014). First, critics have noted that performance funding systems are problematic because they focus too narrowly on graduation rates, which are only one of many measures of student success. Second, it has been noted that institutions can circumvent the goals of performance funding policies by simply becoming more selective. Finally, while research has yet to be conducted to see how performance-based systems affect (in)equity in higher education, performance funding systems might use comparison systems that are unfair for campuses that serve large numbers of underserved student populations, thereby potentially exacerbating systemic racial and socioeconomic inequities. In response, some have advocated for policy makers to reconsider the utility of common outcome metrics and intentionally using performance funding to intentionally address racial and ethnic inequities (Jones, 2014).

For-profit institutions of higher education are also receiving increased attention in postsecondary education policy arenas. The for-profit sector consists of institutions that generate financial profits by providing students with knowledge and skills that fill market demands and college degrees and certificates (Deming, Claudia, & Katz, 2012; Dill, 2005; Hentschke, Lechuga, & Tierney, 2010). On one hand, advocates of for-profit institutions argue that these organizations play a critical role in providing historically underserved students with access to postsecondary opportunities, suggesting that for-profit colleges might be one mechanism to advance racial equity in higher education (Harding, 2010). On the other hand, critics of the for-profit sector have critiqued these institutions for using unethical and aggressive marketing tactics, causing students to assume larger debt levels than their nonprofit counterparts, and providing a low-quality education and fewer returns for the students whom they serve (Iloh & Toldson, 2013; Institute for Higher Education Policy, 2002; Lee, 2012). If disproportionately large numbers of college students of color are enrolling in for-profit colleges and leaving higher education with greater debt and fewer tangible skills, it could be hypothesized that these institutions might be exacerbating already-existing racial inequities in college opportunity.

In sum, it can be argued that racism continues to shape higher education policy in the 21st century. In the following sections, we delineate the ways in which racism shapes individual faculty and student experiences in higher education. It is important to note that people of color can experience each form of racism outlined herein directly or vicariously (Truong, Museus, & McGuire, 2015).

Racism in the Experiences of Higher Education Faculty

Despite the espoused value of diversity in higher education, faculty of color continue to be significantly underrepresented on college campuses. For example, in 2011, only 19% of all full-time faculty members across the nation were Asian American, Black, Latina or Latino, or Pacific Islander (National

Center for Education Statistics [NCES], 2013). While small gains in the representation of persons of color among college faculty have been made in recent years, these gains have primarily been due to increases of persons of color in nontenured instructor ranks (Poloma, 2014; Snyder & Dillow, 2012).

Indeed, it is important to note that the share of faculty who are of color decreases as professorial rank increases. While faculty of color represented just over 25% of assistant professors in 2011, only approximately 21% of associate professors and 16% of full professors were people of color (NCES, 2013). While some might argue that this is a phenomenon unique to predominantly White four-year institutions, there is evidence that community colleges also struggle with maintaining a diverse faculty (Levin, Walker, Jackson-Boothby, & Haberler, 2013).

In this section, we discuss some of the ways in which racism might contribute to the underrepresentation of people of color at the professoriate. Specifically, we outline six themes that emerge from the literature on the racialized experiences of faculty of color: (1) racism in the academic pipeline, (2) racial resistance to faculty authority and expertise, (3) racial hostility in the classroom, (4) racial scrutiny of faculty research agendas, (5) racial taxation from excess faculty service, and (6) racial marginalization and isolation among faculty of color.

Racism in the Academic Pipeline

While many colleges and universities espouse a commitment to diversity, one test of whether that value is enacted at an institution is to examine their efforts at the recruitment, hiring, career development, promotion, and success of professors of color (Jackson & O'Callaghan, 2009). The chronic underrepresentation of people of color in academic positions suggests few institutions have passed this test.

Indeed, evidence points to the reality that institutions often do not make concerted efforts at recruiting, hiring, and retaining faculty of color (Carmen, 1999; Turner, 2003; Turner, Garcia, Nora, & Rendon, 1996). Moreover, it has been noted that faculty recruitment and hiring processes are permeated with racial myths about the lack of qualified applicants. Institutions often relinquish responsibility for their lack of diversity in candidate pools and new hires by claiming an insufficient supply of qualified candidates of color or low demand for academic jobs among candidates of color. Data and evidence, however, do not support such claims. While many graduate students of color depart the pipeline to academic careers at some stage in their trajectory (Turner, Myers, & Creswell, 1999), research suggests that many PhDs of color constitute an untapped resource. On the demand side, dominant narratives suggest that PhDs of color will be unlikely to pursue academic careers given that the accompanying salaries are incomparable to corporate earnings and the private sector may be more welcoming of diversity (Tierney & Sallee, 2008; Trower & Chait, 2002; Turner et al., 1999).

Both the supply and demand explanations of higher education institutions' inability to recruit and hire persons of color suggest that the lack of diversity among the professoriate and administration is the fault of people of color for weeding themselves out of contention for careers in academia. Such self-deterministic narratives blame the victim while insufficiently acknowledging the responsibility and culpability of institutions of higher education in perpetuating the persisting racial inequities in the academic pipeline.

It should also be noted that, once faculty of color land positions in the professoriate, there is some evidence that they may encounter a glass ceiling. Researchers, for example, have noted that White assistant professors are significantly more likely to be promoted to associate or full professor than their Asian American, Black, and Latina or Latino peers (Palepu et al., 1995). There is also some existing evidence that, when controlling for a range of variables such as other demographics and research productivity level, faculty of color are still less likely to attain tenured positions in the academy (Yan & Museus, 2013). Moreover, when controlling for a variety of variables, including faculty demographics and productivity level, faculty of color earn lower salaries than their White counterparts (Lee, 2002).

Racial Resistance to Authority and Expertise

Research suggests that faculty of color report facing covert and overt racial discrimination in the classroom. Challenges to the authority of faculty of color may begin on the first day of class with students questioning their expertise or refusing to call them by their titles (e.g., Professor, Dr., etc.) while simultaneously using these titles to address their White colleagues (Chesler & Young, 2007; Patton & Catching, 2009; Stanley, 2006; Tuitt, Hanna, Martinez, Salazar, & Griffin, 2009). Faculty of color sometimes contend that race plays a role in the ways in which students address them because they are not afforded the same levels of respect as their White colleagues. The following composite story illustrates the experiences of faculty of color:

> *I have come to understand that I do not have the privilege of walking into a classroom and having students assume that I am a capable and credible teacher. Nor do I have the privilege of walking into a classroom and having people assume that I have earned my position through hard work and determination. I have to be deliberate in the subject matter that I teach so that others do not see me as an exception to their assumptions about who is qualified, about who has a right to be here. (Tuitt et al., p. 69)*

Many faculty of color in higher education also express having to work to avoid fitting into stereotypes and doing whatever they can to not be perceived as the "Affirmative Action hire" (Griffin, Ward, & Phillips, 2014; Trower, 2003). When issues of racism emerged in a course, faculty of color often report that their students question their academic integrity and make assumptions that they are biased (Perry, Moore, Edwards, Acosta, & Frey, 2009; Stanley, 2006). Unsurprisingly, then, challenges to the authority of faculty of color are particularly evident when faculty of color teach courses that address racial issues. In these courses, students can resist learning from faculty of color by attempting to discredit them or by pushing back on their inclusion of diversity in the course curriculum (Perry et al., 2009; Stanley, 2006). There is some indication that this resistance could be more likely among predominantly White students who have little prior contact with people of color, particularly persons of color with authority (Perry et al., 2009; Stanley, 2006). In these situations, faculty of color can be forced to respond by asserting their authority by setting firm ground rules for the classroom, being keenly aware of their attire on teaching days, identifying resources outside of the classroom to bolster their credibility, and discussing their credentials for teaching the course subject matter (Chesler & Young, 2007; Perry et al., 2009).

Racial Hostility in the Classroom

While challenging the authority of faculty of color often takes the form of subtle resistance to curricula and pedagogy, some faculty of color experienced more direct and overt forms of discrimination in the classroom that manifest in blatant disrespect, disruption, hostile language, and the like. Indeed, there is some evidence that faculty of color are more likely than their White colleagues to experience disrespect from students in the classroom (Alberts, Hazen, & Theobald, 2010). For example, in a qualitative examination of student interactions with African American faculty, Neville and Parker (2014) observed White college students arriving to class late without apology, texting, and talking in class, arguing with professors, rolling their eyes, and mouthing profanities toward faculty of color. Moreover, it is important to note that White students may become particularly disruptive when they feel the instructor or curriculum challenges their personal beliefs (Collier & Powell, 1990; Jackson & Crawley, 2003; Neville & Parker, 2014).

The aforementioned racial dynamics can have real implications for the careers of faculty of color as these behaviors may further manifest in negative teaching evaluations. Existing studies show that many faculty of color are more likely than their White counterparts to receive negative evaluations (Hamermesh & Parker 2005; Vargas 2002). Moreover, faculty of color who bring more diversity into their teaching seem to be most vulnerable to more negative teaching evaluations (Vargas, 2002). One African American faculty member in Perry et al.'s (2009) investigation, for example, was so concerned about receiving low student evaluations that she decided to stop teaching diversity-related courses. In addition to formal written course evaluations, students sometimes express concerns about the teaching methods and academic integrity of faculty of color to senior faculty and administrators. Coupled with low teaching evaluations, such critiques may negatively impact people's perceptions of faculty of color and their chances of tenure and promotion.

It is important to note that women of color are subject to hostility in the classroom that stems from both racism and sexism (Alberts et al., 2010; Pittman, 2010). As a result, women faculty of color can feel threatened and intimidated by White male students in particular. In one study, for example, Women faculty of color specifically reported that White male students often challenged their scholarly expertise and authority to evaluate them, which led to these students challenging their grades (Pittman, 2010). In that inquiry, students, who were often White males, used threatening tones with women faculty of color, threw papers at them, and in one case a student threatened to "squash" African Americans in efforts to intimidate women faculty of color by espousing White superiority over them.

Racial Scrutiny of Research Agendas

It has been noted that the legitimacy of faculty of color research agendas is also scrutinized if they include a focus on diversity. Because many mainstream journals are less amenable to scholarship on race-related research, faculty of color may choose to find a more welcoming environment to publish in less mainstream academic journals. Indeed, it has been argued that faculty of color are at the forefront of new and progressive journals, including developing new journals, that provide important publication outlets for scholarly agendas that differ from the mainstream (Turner, 2003). In many cases, however, publishing in these journals, while fitting for their scholarly interests, is likely to benefit them less than publishing in mainstream journals in the tenure and promotion process.

Because of the reality that upper ranks of the professoriate are fairly racially homogenous, faculty of color are often evaluated by predominantly White senior faculty personnel committees. When these committees review scholarship in "nonmainstream" journals as part of tenure and promotion portfolios, it may be undervalued, considered too biased to constitute real scholarship, and denigrated as nontraditional or inferior research (Delgado Bernal, 2002; Stanley, 2006; Turner et al., 1999). When personnel review committees maintain a Eurocentric epistemology in the evaluation of faculty of color scholarship, it can create "an apartheid of knowledge" that subordinates the knowledge of faculty of color to mainstream ways of knowing (Delgado Bernal & Villalpando, 2002, p. 175).

Racial Taxation From Excess Service

Faculty of color are often engaged in service commitments that involve mentoring students and junior faculty of color, as well as serving on diversity committees at the institutional, regional, or national levels, and serving their local communities in their educational efforts (Stanley, 2006). While research and teaching may be considered by many to be the most important parts of the three pillars of the professoriate at most institutions of higher education, service has important implications for faculty success. While too much service may negatively impact research productivity, service contributions may be one of few things that provide faculty of color with inspiration and passion, as they desire to serve the communities from which they come or of which they are a part (Turner, Gonzalez, & Wood, 2008).

Unfortunately, though, many faculty of color experience periods of cultural taxation, or what we call racial taxation herein, where they might be consistently bombarded with requests to serve the institution through participation on committees, organization of events, and so on (Padilla, 1994). At the same time, such service is rarely recognized or rewarded by senior faculty or administration during personnel reviews, especially if commitments are related to racial/ethnic diversity. Many faculty of color are therefore caught in a Catch-22 situation, in which they recognize a substantial need for service at their institutions and within their communities, yet this activity results in less time to do research that is more highly valued in promotion and tenure processes (Stanley, 2006; Turner, 2002; Turner et al., 1999). Therefore, existing evidence suggests that faculty of color are forced to balance the pressures to do disproportionately larger amounts of service than their White counterparts with maintaining a robust research agenda to attain promotion and tenure in the academy (Turner, 2002).

Racial Marginalization and Isolation

Faculty of color often experience feelings of marginalization and isolation on campus (Aguirre & Martinez, 1993; Benjamin, 1997; Hune & Chan, 1997;

Padilla & Chavez Chavez, 1995; Smith, 2004). This reality is partly due to the fact that many campuses still employ relatively few faculty of color. Being one of few people of color on a college campus or within an academic department leaves faculty of color vulnerable to racism within their institutions (Garrison-Wade, Diggs, Estrada, & Galindo, 2012). And, racialized structures and practices can, in turn, reinforce "a cycle of exclusion" for many faculty of color (Delgado Bernal & Villalpando, 2002, p. 247).

The Role of Racism in the Experiences of College Students

Minoritized students in college are significantly less likely than White peers to be satisfied with their respective college environments and the overall college experience (Kuh, 2005). In this section, we provide an overview of the ways in which racism shapes the experiences of college students of color. Specifically, we delineate seven themes from the literature regarding how racism shapes the experiences of minoritized college students: (1) racial hostility, (2) racial prejudice and stereotypes, (3) racial invisibility and silencing, (4) racial balkanization or segregation, (5) cultural conflict and dissonance, (6) contradictory cultural pressures, and (7) cultural marginalization and isolation.

Racial Hostility

Evidence suggests that college students of color encounter explicit and implicit forms of racial discrimination. Regarding overt forms of discrimination, this evidence indicates that students of color often encounter racial harassment in college (Ancis, Sedlacek, & Mohr, 2000; Cress & Ikeda, 2003; Feagin, Vera, & Imani, 1996; Hurtado, 1992; Kim, Chang, & Park, 2009; Kotori & Malaney, 2003; Museus & Park, 2015; Museus & Truong, 2013; Smith et al., 2007). The literature illuminates a wide range of ways in which this hostility manifests, including in racial profiling from police, racial slurs, and racial bullying. Sometimes, this harassment can turn violent and lead to racially motivated hate crimes, such as murder (Museus, 2013a). Moreover, it is important to note that, compared to White students, students of color are more likely to experience racial harassment from both faculty and peers on their college campuses (Ancis et al., 2000; Kim et al., 2009; Kotori & Malaney, 2003).

Racial Prejudice and Stereotypes

The literature illuminates many examples of the ways in which students of color experience prejudicial treatment and stereotyping in college (Ancis et al., 2000; Cabrera, 2014; Feagin et al., 1996; Fries-Britt & Turner, 2001; Museus, 2008; Museus & Park, 2015; Museus & Truong, 2013; Smedley, Myers, & Harrell, 1993; Suzuki, 1977, 2002). Academically, Asian American students are often overgeneralized as a model minority that achieves universal and unparalleled academic and occupational success (Suzuki, 1977, 2002). While this model minority myth is benign on the surface, scholars have noted how closer examination of this stereotype reveals many negative consequences for Asian American students (Cheryan & Bodenhausen, 2000; Museus 2013b; Museus & Park, 2015; Suzuki, 2002). For example, it masks the challenges and inequities that exist within that community, places expectations on Asian Americans not to use support services, leads to excessive pressure to achieve perfection among these students, and is used as a tool to argue that racial discrimination is something that can be overcome by hard work and is not deterministic. Asian American men are socially stereotyped as asexual, inferior, submissive, and awkward, while Asian American women are racialized as exotic and sexually submissive—both of which can have significant harmful and sometimes violent racial, social, and psychological consequences (Museus & Truong, 2013b).

Academically, Black and Latina or Latino students often encounter racial stereotypes that they are unprepared or academically inferior, do not deserve to be in college, and only were admitted to college because of affirmative action (Fries-Britt & Turner, 2001; Lewis, Chesler, & Forman, 2000; Museus, 2008; Steele, 1999). Southeast Asian Americans and Pacific Islanders, who tend to come from some of the most underresourced communities and have relatively low educational attainment rates, also face these stereotypes (Museus, 2013b; Ngo & Lee, 2007). Black, Latina or Latino, Native American, Southeast Asian American, and Pacific Islander men can be socially stereotyped as deviant, dropouts, gang members, and dangerous (Feagin et al., 1996).

These racialized stereotypes can also be harmful, and have been one of the reasons cited for the increasingly common media stories of excessive police violence toward Black men across the United States (Correll, Park, Judd, & Wittenbrink, 2007).

Racial Invisibility and Silencing

Evidence also indicates that students of color often find themselves invisible in various spaces on college campuses (Buenavista & Chen, 2013; Buenavista et al., 2009; Feagin et al., 1996; Gonzalez, 2003; Museus & Park, 2015). Given many postsecondary institutions' historical legacy of racism, it might not be surprising that college students of color sometimes report finding themselves invisible in physical structures (e.g., artwork, buildings, etc.) on campus (Brown-Nagin et al., 2015; Gonzalez, 2003). In addition, students of color often find voices from their communities silenced in mainstream curricula and pedagogy (Museus & Park, 2015). Such invisibility and silencing can be pervasive and lead to feelings of racial exclusion, isolation, and marginalization throughout the college experience.

Racial Balkanization or Segregation

There is some indication that college students of color report substantial racial segregation on their campuses (Antonio, 2004; Duster, 1991; Museus & Park, 2015). Indeed, college students of color appear to be very aware that racial segregation is prevalent at their institutions (Antonio, 2004). And, while such segregation can lead to claims that students of color are unwilling to interact outside of their own communities, there is some evidence that students of color gravitate toward peers of similar racial backgrounds in order to find a safe space within larger and less welcoming campus environments (Museus, 2013; Museus & Park, 2015).

It is also important to note that, while students of color do observe racially segregated environments on their college campuses, many White and minoritized students also experience valuable interactions across race that lead to a plethora of positive outcomes (Antonio, 2001; Antonio et al., 2004; Chang, Astin, & Kim, 2004; Chang, Denson, Saenz, & Misa, 2006; Denson, 2009; Denson & Chang, 2009; Jayakumar, 2008; Pike & Kuh, 2006). Therefore, it is important for higher education leaders not to overestimate the level of segregation that occurs on college campuses, because evidence suggests that balkanization prohibits fruitful interracial interactions and positive educational outcomes.

Cultural Dissonance

College students of color also discuss experiencing cultural dissonance as they adjust to and navigate postsecondary institutions. The term *cultural dissonance* refers to the tensions students of color experience as a result of the incongruence between their cultural backgrounds or meaning-making systems and the new cultures that they encounter in their college environment (Museus, 2008). Therefore, many students of color who attend postsecondary institutions with cultures that reflect the cultural values, beliefs, and perspectives of the White majority—which includes most colleges and universities throughout the nation—are likely to confront cultures that are substantially different from the cultures of their home communities and experience significant levels of cultural dissonance in college. Moreover, the levels of cultural dissonance that students experience within their respective college environments are positively associated with cultural stress and likelihood of disengaging from the dominant cultures of their campuses (Museus, 2008; Museus & Park, 2015; Museus & Quaye, 2009).

Contradictory Cultural Pressures

Racialized campus cultures can lead to contradictory pressures for students of color in higher education. Specifically, minoritized college students have reported experiencing significant pressures to assimilate into the cultures of their campuses on one hand (Duster, 1991; Lewis et al., 2000; Museus & Park, 2015), while experiencing pressure to conform to stereotypes of their racial groups that otherize them as distinctly different from the White majority on their campuses. In addition, these conflicting pressures can cause students of color to experience internal conflicts regarding whether and how they can and should conform to or resist the dominant cultures of their respective postsecondary institutions.

Cultural Marginalization and Isolation

Minoritized college students also report experiencing cultural isolation within their respective college cultures (Lewis et al., 2000; Museus & Park, 2015; Turner, 1994). This marginalization and isolation in multiple ways on college campuses. For example, students of color express discontent with the reality that they are structurally marginalized within their campus environments (e.g., the isolation of diversity activity to a single cultural center). In addition, within the larger campus environment, minoritized college students sometimes report feeling like they are the only one on their campuses and in their classrooms. Similarly, minoritized college students sometimes report feeling isolated within mainstream campus subcultures, such as campus-wide student leadership councils or Greek life (Park, 2008).

Conclusion

The scholarship reviewed in this chapter illuminates many of the ways that racism manifests in both higher education policy and the daily experiences of faculty and students of color. Knowledge of these experiences is critical in developing an understanding of the ways in which racism operates within higher education. However, we believe it is important that advocates of racial equity do not become overly focused on these daily experiences but also maintain a focus on the systemic ways in which racism operates and must be addressed. In the following chapter, we argue that racial justice advocates in higher education should focus on systemic forms of racial oppression in racial discourse and their efforts to advance toward racial equity.

Advancing Scholarship and Advocacy to Achieve Equity in Higher Education

I N THE FIRST CHAPTER, "Introduction," we discuss important demographic realities within U.S. society and highlight persistent racial inequalities throughout the nation. In doing so, we underscore the urgency of
understanding and addressing systemic racism throughout our system of
higher education. In the second chapter, "Racial Frameworks in Higher Education," we provide an overview of a handful of race-conscious frameworks
that can be used to understand racial problems in higher education today
and begin to address them meaningfully. We believe that this chapter highlights the reality that, although much work in this area remains to be done,
higher education has made significant progress with regard to generating useful tools that can be engaged to spark major transformation toward greater
racial equity in higher education. In the third chapter, "Historical and Contemporary Racial Contexts," we provide an overview of the historical roots of
racism and U.S. society. We also examine how racism has historically shaped
events and policies that have been critical to the development of the higher
education system in the United States. Through this discussion, we underscore the embedded and pervasive nature of racism throughout society and
social institutions. Such understandings are necessary for higher education
professionals to grasp the gravity of existing racial problems and prepare to
address them. In the fourth chapter, "Systemic Racism in Higher Education,"
we provide an overview of how racism shapes higher education policy and

the experiences of individuals within institutions of higher education. In this concluding chapter, we utilize the frameworks and research from these prior chapters to construct a set of recommendations for higher education policy and practice aimed at advancing racial equity.

The persisting racial disparities in higher education outcomes are indicators that higher education has failed to successfully and sufficiently adapt to student populations that are increasingly racially diverse. In fact, many institutions have been so slow to adapt to these demographic shifts that we fear that higher education, as a system, might be unable or unwilling to effectively respond to the diversity of its student bodies and make the changes necessary to achieve more racially equitable outcomes. Nevertheless, we assert that it is time to rethink higher education's approach to addressing racial inequities and adopt a more holistic and aggressive strategy to advance equity agendas.

Before moving forward with our discussion of what a more holistic and aggressive approach might look like, a few caveats are in order. First, we realize that readers who reject the racial realities shaping our postsecondary education system or devalue efforts to achieve racial equity might find our suggestions problematic. However, we hope that the discussion in the previous chapters offers a convincing case for why such efforts are critical. At the same time, we acknowledge that the points made herein could be perceived as naively idealistic, or even unrealistic, by those who already appreciate the cause of racial equity. We do not contest the notion that our recommendations are idealistic. Nevertheless, we believe that, if we are serious about moving toward greater equity, we must be idealistic and we must be visionary.

Second, we urge caution on the part of racial justice advocates, and call on them to consider the potential unintended consequences of equity work. Over the past few decades, diversity and multiculturalism have been widely espoused by institutions of higher education. Although this development could be viewed as progress among those advocating for racial equity, diversity and multiculturalism have often been adopted in ways that are superficial and do not focus attention and energy on solving real systemic social problems. As such, they can create an illusion that institutions have transcended racial problems and douse any further interest in advancing racial equity even though racism still permeates their policies, curricula, and spaces. In addition, anecdotal evidence suggests that institutions that have adopted campus-wide diversity requirements have simultaneously heard challenges to the need for ethnic studies programs or other programs and services targeted at supporting marginalized populations. These are also examples of how efforts to achieve greater racial equity can cause the system to adapt in ways that hinder those efforts from having transformative impact. Thus, it is imperative that efforts to advance racial equity are informed by the progress already made by minority serving institutions, ethnic studies programs and departments, targeted support programs and services, and ethnic student organizations. Indeed, efforts to achieve greater racial equity should not replace these hotbeds of equity work, but rather must learn from them and leverage them to facilitate broader institutional transformation.

Third, we assert that it is important to acknowledge the value of understanding how racism works *and* how to advance racial equity work. It is common for people to express frustrations with the postsecondary education system or argue that it needs to be changed. However, such frustrations and assertions can fall short of offering new radical and well-developed strategies regarding how higher education systems might be transformed to achieve racial equity. The current volume and discussion are based on the assumption that any broad systemic transformation requires a thoughtful systemic approach. Of course, we acknowledge the reality that there are many cultural and structural challenges to radically and systemically transforming institutions of higher education and advancing racial equity.

Finally, we believe that many higher education scholars, policy makers, and educators throughout the nation are engaging in important and valuable equity work, but these efforts are often confined to silos. In response, we urge postsecondary organizations and educators to enhance their collective impact by constructing a common vision for equity work and collaborating to mobilize and achieve that vision. For example, we wonder what changes could be realized if scholars, policy makers, and practitioners work together to refocus performance funding and accountability discourses, institutional mission statements and strategic plans, and campus programs and practices on cultivating the types of culturally engaging campus environments that allow diverse populations to thrive and in ways that are aligned with the college completion agenda and other larger policy narratives. We do not suggest that such actions are a panacea for higher education's racial problems. However, collectively organizing and mobilizing around such common foci could lead to greater collective impact and a more racially equitable systems.

Advancing Racial Equity in Higher Education Scholarship

As we discuss throughout this volume, the higher education community has generated substantial insights into the ways in which racism shapes higher education systems and experiences within them, but we believe that existing gaps in knowledge still exist and hinder the ability of policymakers and practitioners to advance racial equity goals. For example, higher education scholars have produced noteworthy literature on the problematic nature of campus climates and the challenges that emerge from hostile environments encountered by students of color (see Harper & Hurtado, 2007). Yet, with few exceptions, higher education researchers have failed to develop comprehensive understandings of the types of environments that must be cultivated to ensure that racially diverse populations can thrive in college (Museus, 2014). Similarly, few scholars have helped shed significant light on how postsecondary institutions can be transformed or are being changed to achieve greater racial equity (e.g., Dowd & Bensimon, 2015; Kezar, 2012). Thus, examining the field of higher education from a systems perspective, we believe that the higher education scholarly community still has much to learn about racism and processes to move toward racial equity. As a result, many advocates of racial equity on college and university campuses are ill-equipped with tools and evidence to help them navigate institutional environments with a focus on cultivating optimal institutions for racial equity.

Given the realities above, we believe there is an urgent need to fill the gaps and begin to generate more holistic understandings of both racism and how to inform efforts to achieve racial equity. Moreover, we believe that, in order for the field to generate such comprehensive understandings, it not only needs researchers that study racial problems and issues in higher education broadly, but it also needs more scholars who are racial experts within diverse sectors of the field (e.g., organizational systems, curricular and pedagogical contexts, student affairs units, institutional change processes, etc.). Relatedly, in the coming years, we believe that it is critical that higher education scholars pursue the following areas of inquiry:

- Document the ways in which seemingly objective federal and state policies (e.g., performance funding systems) perpetuate or reinforce systems of racial inequity.
- Understand and cultivate discourse about how to make public policy processes more racially conscious.
- Document the relationship between culturally engaging campus environments and student outcomes.
- Advance knowledge about institutional resistance to cultivating optimally inclusive campus environments in which increasingly diverse student populations can thrive. Specifically, document the types of barriers will they encounter throughout the process, and ways in which such challenges can be addressed.
- Increase discourse on how scholars, policymakers, and practitioners can reframe critical discourses (e.g., the college completion agenda and higher education quality) to make them more racially conscious.
- Advance knowledge regarding how campus structures be reorganized in cost-effective ways to provide minoritized populations with the types of culturally engaging campus supports that they need during college.
- Better document what the process of cultural transformation to achieve more culturally engaging campus environments looks like.
- Examine how institutions can support faculty and staff in developing their racial consciousness and cultivating more racially inclusive environments.
- Document the challenges that faculty encounter as they attempt to transform their curricula and pedagogy to be more racially inclusive. Better understand how faculty can overcome these barriers.
- Illuminate the most effective ways that college campuses can use data to facilitate institutional transformation toward racial equity.
- Analyze the process of bridging gaps between research and policy or research and practice to advance an equity agenda.

In sum, we are advocating higher education scholars to generate greater insights on how racism can be addressed within various aspects of higher education systems. Such knowledge can help generate tools to equip higher education policymakers and practitioners who hope to advance more racially equitable policy and practice.

Advancing Racial Equity in Higher Education Policy

Federal and state governments must play an active role in constructing more equitable higher education systems and eliminating systemic racial and ethnic inequities as well. As we discuss in the second chapter, "Racial Frameworks in Higher Education," history demonstrates that seemingly objective policies can reinforce systems of racial oppression. Thus, in order for higher education policy makers to help improve the system and move toward greater racial equity, they must understand the need for racially conscious policy and intentionally incorporate equity into their policy-making processes.

Performance funding constitutes a case in which higher education policy makers can rethink policy in more racially conscious ways that can help advance their current agendas while simultaneously advocating for racial equity. Specifically, policy makers must recognize that color-blind discourses around college completion and performance funding are problematic. And, they can reframe these discourses to acknowledge that colleges and universities must fundamentally transform to maximize positive outcomes among their increasingly diverse student populations. One way advocates can achieve such reframing is by making efforts to ensure that conversations around performance funding systems are not only based on measures of traditional outputs (e.g., persistence and degree completion rates), but also emphasize metrics to understand whether institutions are cultivating optimal environments that allow students from all racial backgrounds can thrive (Museus, 2014, 2015). Indeed, just as institutions have utilized indicators of student engagement in accrediting processes (McCormick & Kinzie, 2014), states could encourage campuses to utilize indicators of culturally engaging campus environments in their accountability systems (Museus, 2014, 2015).

If the federal government is serious about making opportunity accessible to all students, it must also make higher education institutions more accountable for facilitating more equitable outcomes. Indeed, all campuses that purport to serve a racially and ethnically "diverse" student population must be held accountable for achieving racial equity in college persistence and degree completion rates, learning outcomes, and subsequent employment opportunities. This accountability, however, must be accompanied by resources to help institutions rethink the way that they do business to make their systems more culturally inclusive and ensure that students from racially diverse backgrounds can thrive in college.

MSIs offer one example of how a lack of accountability for racial equity can be problematic. Many historically predominantly White institutions have witnessed the percentage of their student bodies reach the federally designated threshold for MSI designations, and have been granted that status. For example, institutions with enrollment that reaches 25% Latina and Latino students qualify for designation as a Hispanic Serving Institution (HSI). Institutions with enrollment of 10% Asian American and Pacific Islander students qualify for designation as Asian American Native American and Pacific Islander Serving Institutions (AANAPISI). Once an institution meets the MSI status threshold, it is eligible for federal grants to support the implementation of programs to better support students (U.S. Department of Education). However, the federal government requires institutions to prove their effectiveness by reporting improvements in overall success rates, rather than improvement in success rates among the population of color that led to the designation (e.g., Latina and Latino students at Hispanic Serving Institutions). Thus, while many MSIs are utilizing these funds to serve their underserved populations of color, it is important for the federal government to verify that allocated funds used to enhance general programming on campus also improve the experience and outcomes of students of color. Otherwise, the lack of a federal mandate for these programs to demonstrate some benefit to college students of color sends messages to colleges and universities that these students are not a priority and their institutions are not accountable for maximizing their success.

With regard to higher education finance policy, both federal and state governments must address the issue of affordability within higher education if we are to move toward greater racial equity. States must do their part by increasing, rather than reducing, funding for higher education. Indeed, decreases in state support may lead to increases in tuition, further limiting opportunities for students of color. However, if college students of color are more averse to taking out loans, the federal government must also invest in students by shifting the emphasis back to grants, rather than loans, in the composition of financial aid packages. Although such recommendations might sound naively optimistic given recent shifts toward the privatization of higher education, we are hopeful that public policy makers can once again embrace their commitment to education as a public good.

Advancing Racial Equity on College Campuses

Of course, colleges and universities must engage in intentional long-term efforts to achieve racial equity if they are authentically committed to such outcomes. The past two decades of research in higher education offers a plethora of articles that provide recommendations regarding how to implement specific programs and practices to cultivate more inclusive environments to support underserved students and achieve greater racial equity within institutions of higher education. We do not rehash these recommendations, and refer our readers to these prior works for specific actions that can be taken at the institutional, programmatic, and individual levels (e.g., Dowd & Bensimon, 2015; Jayakumar & Museus, 2012; Kezar, 2012; Smith, 2011, 2015). Instead, and in keeping with the systemic focus of the current volume, we offer a broader framework that can help institutions consider how to pursue more systemic efforts to transform the cultures and structures of their campuses and create more equitable postsecondary institutions.

We believe that the preceding discussion, the aforementioned models in particular, provides important elements of a comprehensive approach to pursuing institutional transformation and equity. Building upon and incorporating the work of Delgado and Stefancic (2001), Dowd and Bensimon

FIGURE 7
An Institutional Framework for Racial Justice Advocacy

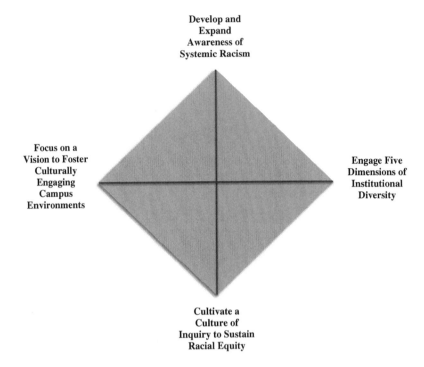

Develop and
Expand
Awareness of
Systemic Racism

Focus on a
Vision to Foster
Culturally
Engaging
Campus
Environments

Engage Five
Dimensions of
Institutional
Diversity

Cultivate a
Culture of
Inquiry to Sustain
Racial Equity

(2015), Museus (2014, 2015), and Smith (2011, 2015), we posit that 21st century racial justice advocacy in higher education necessitates deliberate integration of processes that engage *all* critical aspects of educational organizations. Thus, we offer an institutional framework for racial justice advocacy that was constructed using the aforementioned theories and research (Figure 7). The framework in Figure 7 includes four main components that complement one another and, together, offer a more holistic perspective regarding how campuses can begin to pursue broad and deep systemic transformation in higher education.

1. *Develop and expand awareness of systemic racism:* Campuses must cultivate awareness that racism is endemic to higher education, continues to shape the cultures of postsecondary institutions, and may negatively impact

student, faculty, and staff experiences and outcomes (Delgado & Stenfacic, 2001; Museus, Ravello, et al., 2012). This awareness must go beyond giving adequate attention to overt acts of racism to thoroughly interrogating embedded institutional policies and practices that consciously or inadvertently perpetuate inequities through scholarship, curricula, policies, support structures, and other parts of the campus. For example, we believe that all campus units at every institution should be encouraged to examine their own assumptions about racism, scrutinize existing policies and practices from a racially conscious lens, and consider ways in which their own policies and practices might implicitly reproduce racial inequities. Institutions should be provided support to carry out these investigations, and should be held accountable for making effective changes.

2. *Cultivate cultures of inquiry to achieve equity:* Postsecondary institutions should prioritize the cultivation of a culture of inquiry and problem solving to achieve racial equity (Witham & Bensimon, 2012). Again, the goal to achieve equity includes, but should not be limited to, producing racially equitable student outcomes (e.g., learning outcomes, satisfaction levels, persistence, and degree completion). Racial equity goals should also include aims to transform the cultures and structures of postsecondary institutions to be more racially equitable. These efforts require college and university campuses to make substantial commitments to setting institutional transformation goals, engaging in research and assessment to measure progress toward these goals, and adopting a culture of institutional improvement and equity.

3. *Focus on a vision to foster culturally engaging campus environments:* Institutions of higher education should consider the importance of constructing a common vision to cultivate more culturally engaging campus environments. Such a vision would focus on maximizing the extent to which students have access to environments characterized by cultural familiarity, culturally relevant knowledge, cultural community service, cultural validation, meaningful cross-cultural engagement, collectivism, humanized educational environments, holistic support, and proactive philosophies (Museus, 2014, 2015). Espousing and enacting such a vision require institutions to grapple with difficult questions about how they can diversify

their faculty and staff, restructure student support services, redesign curricula and pedagogy, strengthen their relationships with diverse communities, and engage in other activities that can help transform their academic and social spaces so that they are characterized by inclusive excellence.

4. *Engage the five dimensions of institutional diversity:* Finally, institutions should ensure that the goal of achieving equity and focus on culturally engaging campus environments is embedded within all critical aspects of the institution (Smith, 2011, 2015). Put another way, mission statements—as well as vision statements and strategic plans—across campuses should reflect the goal of equity and focus on culturally engaging campus environments and institutions' capacity and structures to promote more culturally relevant and responsive systems. Scholarship and pedagogy should reflect such culturally engaging characteristics, campus climates should be characterized by diverse groups co-constructing more culturally engaging campus environments, and institutions should aim to ensure access and success to students from diverse backgrounds via the cultivation of such culturally engaging environments.

Each of the four elements of this framework is critical, but not sufficient, to advance racial justice in postsecondary institutions. We present them here, together, as a more holistic lens that can be used to guide institutional transformation efforts to achieve greater equity.

Conclusion

Today, racism is nationally visible. The increasing presence of televised and digitally disseminated incidents depicting racial hostility toward people of color, such as those discussed at the beginning of this monograph, serves as an all too regular backdrop to everyday conversations. At both local and national levels, political and community leaders are wrestling with questions regarding how to make sense of racial inequality in the 21st century. While there are no easy answers to such questions, if higher education is going to truly live up to its idealistic role of promoting social progress and mobility for *all* students regardless of their racial backgrounds, we believe that we must abandon some of the assumptions that drive higher education policy and practice. Federal and state policy makers can no longer advocate for higher persistence and graduation rates without pushing higher education institutions to fundamentally transform to reflect the historically marginalized and growing populations of color entering their campuses. At the same time, postsecondary institutions can no longer superficially commit to vague concepts of diversity, multiculturalism, or equality in mission statements and recruiting materials while failing to do the difficult work of pursuing systemic transformation to create more inclusive environments so that racially diverse populations can thrive. If we are to make significant advances toward racial equity in the 21st century, we must account for the systemic nature of the race problem in higher education, and develop more systemic solutions to it.

Glossary: Key Terms and Definitions Related to Racism and Racial Equity

Aversive racism is the phenomenon of Whites endorsing egalitarian values and regard themselves as nonprejudiced, but discriminating against populations of color in subtle ways that are rationalized (Gaertner & Dovidio, 1986; Sears, 1988).

Colorblind racism: See aversive racism.

Cultural racism results from enthnocentrism and power, and describes how members of society favor the cultural values, beliefs, and norms of the dominant racial group over minority populations. Through this process, minority groups are racialized as inferior, which contributes to the oppression of these populations (Jones, 1997).

Individual racism is the "beliefs, attitudes, and actions of individuals that support or perpetuate racism" (Wijeyesinghe, Griffin, & Love, 1997, p. 89).

Institutional racism is the "patterns, procedures, practices, and policies that operate within social institutions so as to consistently penalize, disadvantage, and exploit individuals who are members of racial minority groups" (Better, 2007, p. 11).

Minoritized is a term that we utilize to refer to people of color. It is based on the assumption that people of color are not inherently racial minorities but that racism operates to force minority status upon them within U.S. society.

Oppression is a system of domination and exploitation of subordinated groups, whereby groups in positions of power and privilege engage in the unjust treatment of subordinated groups and deny the latter access to resources (Gil, 1998).

Racial equity, broadly defined, refers to racially equitable systems in which racially diverse perspectives are equally embedded in power structures, policy-making processes, and the cultural fabric of institutions.

Racial formation is the process by which economic, political, and social forces shape racial categories, the meanings that are associated with those categories, and their value (Omi & Winant, 1994).

Racialization is the process of constructing racial categories, applying these racial labels to previously unclassified groups or practices, and attaching racial meanings to these categories and groups or practices with which they are associated (Omi & Winant, 1994).

Racism is a system of dominance, power, and privilege that is rooted in the historical oppression of subordinated groups that the dominant group views as inferior, deviant, or undesirable. The dominant group creates or maintains structures and ideology that preserve their power and privilege while excluding subjugated groups from power, status, and access to resources (Harrell, 2000).

Secondhand racism is the process by which people of color observe other minoritized persons experiences of racism, and realize that they are also vulnerable to the influence of racism and experience negative ramifications of these observations and conclusions. People of color can either directly and visually observe racism or more indirectly learn about racist incidents via stories from family, friends, community, strangers, or the media (Truong et al., 2015).

Symbolic racism: See aversive racism.

Systemic racism is racism that permeates society and all major social institutions. It functions as a system of social oppression that is deeply embedded and is intensely contested (Feagin, 2006).

Vicarious racism: See secondhand racism.

White supremacy refers to a political, economic, and cultural system through which Whites overwhelmingly control power and resources, conscious and unconscious ideas of White superiority and entitlement are widespread, and White dominance and the subordination of people of color are reinforced daily across a wide range of institutions and social settings (Ansley, 1988).

References

Acuña, R. F. (2014). *Occupied America: A history of Chicanos* (8th ed.). Boston, MA: Pearson.

Aguirre, A., & Martinez, R. O. (1993). *Chicanos in higher education: Issues and dilemmas for the 21st century* (ASHE-ERIC Higher Education Report No. 3). Washington, DC: ERIC Clearinghouse on Higher Education, George Washington University, in cooperation with the Association for the Study of Higher Education.

Alberts, H. C., Hazen, H. D. & Theobald, R. B. (2010). Classroom incivilities: The challenge of interactions between college students and instructors in the U.S. *Journal of Geography in Higher Education, 34*(3), 439–462.

Ancis, J. R., Sedlacek, W. E., & Mohr, J. (2000). Student perceptions of campus cultural climate by race. *Journal of Counseling and Development, 78*(2), 180–185.

Ansley, F. L. (1988). Stirring the ashes: Race class and the future of Civil Rights scholarship. *Cornell Law Review, 74*, 993–1077.

Antonio, A. L. (2001). The role of inter-racial interaction in the development of leadership skills and cultural knowledge and understanding. *Research in Higher Education, 42*(5), 593–617.

Antonio, A. L. (2004). Diversity and the influence of friendship groups in college. *The Review of Higher Education, 25*(1), 63–89.

Antonio, A. L., Chang, M. J., Hakuta, K., Kenny, D. A., Levin, S., & Milem, J. F. (2004). Effects of racial diversity on complex thinking in college students. *Psychological Science, 15*(8), 507–510.

Astin, A. W. (1993). *What matters in college? Four critical years revisited.* San Francisco, CA: Jossey-Bass.

Atkinson, R. C., & Geiser, S. (2009). Reflections on a century of college admissions tests. *Educational Researcher, 38*(9), 665–676.

Au, W. (2009). Unequal by design. *High-stakes testing and the standardization of inequality.* London, England: Routledge.

Barrett, D., Vilensky, M., & Jackson, J. (2014, December 4). New York City police officer won't face criminal charges in Eric Garner death. *The Wall Street Journal.*

Bauer, K. (Ed.). (1998). *Campus climate: Understanding the critical components of today's colleges and universities.* New Directions for Institutional Research (No. 98). San Francisco, CA: Jossey-Bass.

Bell, D. A. (1980). *Brown v. Board of Education* and the Interest-Convergence Dilemma. *Harvard Law Review, 93,* 518–533.

Bell, D. A. (1987). *And we are not saved.* New York, NY: Basic Books.

Bell, D. A. (1989). *And we are not saved: The elusive quest for racial justice.* New York, NY: Basic Books.

Bell, D. A. (1992). *Faces at the bottom of the well: The permanence of racism.* New York, NY: Basic Books.

Bell, D. A. (2004). *Silent covenants: Brown v. Board of Education and the unfulfilled hopes for racial reform.* New York, NY: Oxford University Press.

Bell, D. A. (2005a). The unintended lessons in *Brown v. Board of Education. New York Law School Law Review, 49,* 1053–1067.

Bell, D. A. (2005b). Racial realism. In R. Delgado & J. Stefancic (Eds.), *The Derrick Bell reader* (pp. 55–96). New York, NY: Oxford University Press.

Banaji, M. R. (2001). Implicit attitudes can be measured. In H. L. Roediger III, J. S. Nairne, & A. Suprenant (Eds.), *The nature of remembering: Essays in honor of Robert G. Crowder* (pp. 117–150). Washington, DC: American Psychological Association.

Benjamin, L. (Ed.). (1997). *Black women in the academy: Promises and perils.* Gainesville: University Press of Florida.

Bensimon, E.M., & Malcolm, L. (Eds.). (2012). *Confronting equity issues on campus: Implementing the equity scorecard in theory and practice.* Sterling, VI: Stylus.

Better, S. (2007). *Institutional racism: A primer on theory and strategies for social change.* Boulder, CO: Rowman & Littlefield.

Bidwell, A. (2015, March 10). Opt-out movement about more than tests, advocates say. *U.S. News and World Report.* Retrieved from http://www.usnews.com/news/articles/2015/03/10/as-students-opt-out-of-common-core-exams-some-say-movement-is-not-about-testing

Blaut, J. M. (1993). *The colonizer's model of the world: Geographic diffusionism and Eurocentric history.* New York: Guilford Press.

Bok, D. (2013). *Higher education in America.* Princeton, NJ: Princeton University Press.

Bond, H. M. (1924). What the army "intelligence tests" measured. In R. Jacoby & N. Glauberman (Eds.), *The bell curve debate: History, documents, opinions* (pp. 583–598). New York: Times Books.

Bonilla-Silva, E. (2003). *Racism without racists: Color-blind racism and the persistence of racial inequality in the United States.* Lanham, MD: Rowman & Littlefield.

Bonner II, F. A., Marbley, A. F., Tuitt, F., Robinson, P. A., Banda, R. M., & Hughes, R. L. (2014). *Black faculty in the academy: Narratives for negotiating identity and achieving career success.* New York: Routledge.

Bowen, W., & Bok, D. (1998). *The shape of the river: The long-term consequences of considering race in college and university admissions.* Princeton, NJ: Princeton University Press.

Brack, M. B. (1970). Mexican opinion, American racism, and the War of 1846. *The Western Historical Quarterly, 1*(2), 161–174.

Brayboy, B. M. J. (2005). Toward a tribal critical race theory in education. *The Urban Review, 37*(5), 425–446.

Brown v. Board of Education, 347 U.S. 483 (1954).

Brooks, D. (2015, May 1). The nature of poverty. *Washington Post.* Retrieved from http://www.nytimes.com/2015/05/01/opinion/david-brooks-the-nature-of-poverty.html

Brown, D. (1990). Racism and race relations in the university. *Virginia Law Review, 76,* 295–335.

Brown-Nagin, T., Guinier, L., & Torres, G. (2015). Tejas es diferente: UT Austin's admissions program in light of its exclusionary history. In U. M. Jayakumar & L. M. Garces (Eds.) with F. Fernandez, *Affirmative action and racial equity: Considering the* Fisher *case to forge a path ahead* (pp. 63–79). New York, NY: Routledge.

Brubacher, J. S. & Rudy, W. (1997). *Higher education in transition: A history of American colleges and universities.* Piscataway, NJ: Transaction.

Buenavista, T. L., & Chen, A. C. (2013). Intersections and crossroads: A counter-story of an undocumented Pinay college student. In S. D. Museus, D. Maramba, & R. Teranishi (Eds.), *The misrepresented minority: New insights on Asian Americans and Pacific Islanders, and their implications for higher education.* Sterling, VA: Stylus.

Buenavista, T. L., Jayakumar, U. M., & Misa-Escalante, K. (2009). Contextualizing Asian American education through critical race theory: An example of U.S. Pilipino college student experiences. In S. D. Museus (Ed.), *Conducting research on Asian Americans in higher education.* New Directions for Institutional Research (No. 142, pp. 69–81). San Francisco, CA: Jossey-Bass.

Burnham, L. B. (2009). *Changing the race: Racial politics and the election of Barack Obama.* New York, NY: Applied Research Center.

Cabrera, N. L. (2014). But we're not laughing: White male college students' racial joking and what this says about "post-racial" discourse. *Journal of College Student Development, 55*(1), 1–15.

Calmore, J. (1992). Critical race theory, Archie Shepp, and fire music: Securing an authentic intellectual life in a multicultural world. *Southern California Law Review, 65,* 2129–2231.

Carcamo, C. (2013, March 12). Governor of Arizona banned ethnic studies in Tucson. *Los Angeles Times.* Retrieved from http://articles.latimes.com/2013/mar/12/nation/la-na-nn-ff-ethnic-studies-arizona-20130312

Carey, K. (2004). *A matter of degrees: Improving graduation rates in four-year colleges and universities.* Washington, DC: The Education Trust.

Carey, K. (2005). *One step from the finish line: Higher college completion rates are within our reach.* Washington, DC: The Education Trust.

Carmen, F. (1999). *In their own voice: The experiences of counselor educators of color in academe* (Unpublished doctoral dissertation). University of New Mexico.

Carrigan, W. D., & Web, C. (2003). The lynching of persons of Mexican origin or descent in the United States, 1848–1928. *The Journal of Social History, 37*(2), 413–438.

Carter Andrews, D. J., & Tuitt, F. (2013). *Contesting the myth of a "post racial" era: The continued significance of race in U.S. education.* New York: Peter Lang.

Castagno, A. E., & Lee, S. J. (2007). Native mascots and ethnic fraud in higher education: Using tribal critical race theory and the interest convergence principle as an analytic tool. *Equity & Excellence in Education, 40*(1), 3–13.

Centers for Disease Control and Prevention (2011). *CDC health disparities and inequalities report.* Washington, DC: Author.

Chan, S. (1991). *Asian Americans: An interpretive history.* Boston, MA: Twayne.

Chang, M. J., Astin, A. W., & Kim, D. (2004). Cross-racial interaction among undergraduates: Some consequences, causes, and patterns. *Research in Higher Education, 45*(5), 529–553.

Chang, M. J., Chang, J. C. & Ledesma, M. C. (2005). Beyond magical thinking: Doing the real work of diversifying our institutions. *About Campus*, 9–16.

Chang, M. J., Denson, D., Saenz, V., & Misa, K. (2006). The educational benefits of sustaining cross-racial interaction among undergraduates. *Journal of Higher Education*, 77(3), 430–455.

Chang, R. S. (1993). Towards and Asian American legal scholarship: Critical Race Theory, post-structuralism, and narrative space. *California Law Review*, 81(5), 1243–1323.

Cheryan, S., & Bodenhausen, G. V. (2000). When positive stereotypes threaten intellectual performance: The psychological hazards of "model minority" status. *Psychological Science*, 11, 399–402.

Chesler, M. & Young, A. (2007). Faculty members' social identities and classroom authority. *Scholarship of multicultural teaching and learning*. New Directions for Teaching and Learning (No. 11, pp. 11–19). San Francisco, CA: Jossey-Bass.

Chon, M. (1995). On the need for Asian American narratives in law: Ethnic specimens, native informants, storytelling and silences. *UCLA Asian Pacific American Law Journal*, 3, 4–32.

Cohen, A. M. (1998). *The shaping of American higher education: Emergence and growth if the contemporary system*. San Francisco, CA: Jossey-Bass.

College Board (2014). *Trends in college pricing, 2014*. Washington, DC: Author.

Collier, M. J., & Powell, R. (1990). Ethnicity, instructional communication and classroom systems. *Communication Quarterly*, 38(4), 334–349.

Correll, J., Park, B., Judd, C. M., & Wittenbrink, A. B. (2007). The influence of stereotypes on decisions to shoot. *European Journal of Social Psychology*, 37, 1102–1117.

Covarrubias, P. O., & Windchief, S. R. (2009). Silences in Stewardship: Some American Indian College Students Examples. *The Howard Journal of Communications*, 20(4), 333–352.

Crenshaw, K. (1989). Demarginalizing the intersection of race and sex: A Black feminist critique of antidiscrimination doctrine, feminist theory and antiracist politics. *University of Chicago Legal Forum*, 1989, 139–167.

Crenshaw, K. (1993). Mapping the margins: Intersectionality, identity politics, and the violence against women of color. *Stanford Law Review*, 43, 1241–1299.

Crenshaw, K. W. (2011). Twenty years of Critical Race theory: Looking back to more forward. *Connecticut Law Review*, 43(5), 1253–1353.

Crenshaw, K., Gotanda, N., Peller, G., & Thomas, K. (Eds.). (1995). *Critical race theory: The key writings that formed the movement*. New York, NY: New Press.

Cress, C. M., & Ikeda, E. K. (2003). Distress under duress: The relationship between campus climate and depression in Asian American college students. *NASPA Journal*, 40(2), 74–97.

Darder, A., & Torres, R. D. (2004). *After race: Racism after multiculturalism*. New York, NY: New York University Press.

Davey, M., & Bossman, J. (2014, November 12). Protests flare after Ferguson police officer is not indicted. *New York Times*.

Delgado, R. (1984). The imperial scholar: Reflections on a review of civil rights literature. *University of Pennsylvania Law Review*, 132, 561–578.

Delgado, R. (1989). Storytelling for oppositionists and others: A plea for narrative. *Michigan Law Review*, 87, 2411–2441.

Delgado, R. (1992). The imperial scholar revisited: How to marginalize outsider writing, ten years later. *University of Pennsylvania Law Review*, 140, 1349–1372.

Delgado, R. (2009). The law of the noose: A history of Latino lynchings. *Harvard Civil Rights-Civil Liberties Law Review, 44*, 297–312.

Delgado, R., & Stefancic, J. (2001). *Critical race theory: An introduction*. New York, NY: New York University Press.

Delgado Bernal, D. (2002). Critical race theory, Latino critical theory, and critical raced gendered epistemologies: Recognizing students of color as holders and creators of knowledge. *Qualitative Inquiry, 8*, 105–126.

Delgado Bernal, D., & Villalpando, O. (2002). An apartheid of knowledge in academia: the struggle over the "legitimate" knowledge of faculty of color. *Equity and Excellence in Education, 35*(2), 169–180.

Deming, D., Claudia, G., & Katz, L. F. (2012). The for-profit postsecondary school sector: Nimble critters or agile predators? *Journal of Economic Perspectives, 26*, 139–164.

Denson, N. (2009). Do curricular and cocurricular diversity activities influence racial bias? A meta-analysis. *Review of Educational Research, 79*(2), 805–838.

Denson, N., & Chang, M. J. (2009). Racial diversity matters: The impact of diversity-related student engagement and institutional context. *American Educational Research Journal, 46*(2), 322–353.

DeVos, T., & Banaji, M. R. (2005). American = White? *Journal of personality and social psychology, 88*, 447–466.

Dill, D. D. (2005, April). *The public good, the public interest, and public higher education*. Paper prepared for the Conference Recapturing the "Public" in Public Higher Education, Graduate Center, City University of New York. Retrieved from http://www.unc.edu/ppaq/docs/PublicvsPrivate.pdf

Dixson, A. D., & Rousseau, C. K. (2005). And we are still not saved: Critical Race theory in education ten years later. *Race Ethnicity and Education, 8*(1), 7–27.

Dovidio, J. F., Gaertner, S. L., Kawakami, K., & Hodson, G. (2002). Why can't we just get along? Interpersonal biases and interracial distrust. *Cultural diversity and Ethnic Minority Psychology, 8*(2), 88–102.

Dowd, A. C., & Bensimon, E. M. (2015). *Engaging the "race question": Accountability and equity in U.S. higher education*. New York, NY: Teachers College Press.

Du Bois, W. E. B. (1926). Negroes in college. In E. F. Provenzo Jr. (Ed.), *Du Bois on education* (pp. 235–241). Walnut Creek, CA: AltaMira Press.

Du Bois, W. E. B. (1935). Does the Negro need separate schools? In E. J. Sundquist (Ed.), *The Oxford W. E. B. Du Bois Reader* (pp. 423–431). New York, NY: Oxford University Press.

Dudley, M. K. (1990). *A Hawaiian nation I: Man, gods, and nature*. Honolulu, HI: Nā Kāne O Ka Malo Press.

Duster, T. (1991). *The diversity project: Final report*. Berkeley: Institute for the Study of Social Change, University of California, Berkeley.

Espino, M. M., Muñoz, S. M., & Kiyama, J. M. (2010). Transitioning from doctoral study to the academy: Theorizing trenzas of identity for Latina sister scholars. *Qualitative Inquiry, 16*(10), 804–818.

Espinoza, L., & Harris, A. P. (1997). Afterword: Embracing the tar-baby. LatCrit Theory and the sticky mess of race. *California Law Review, 85*(5), 1585–1645.

Espiritu. (1993). *Asian American panethnicity: Bridging institutions and identities*. Philadelphia, PA: Temple University Press.

Espiritu, Y. L. (2008). *Asian American women and men: Labor, laws, and love* (2nd ed.). Lanham, MD: Rowman & Littlefield Publishers, Inc.

Feagin, J. R. (2006). *Systemic racism: A theory of oppression.* New York, NY: Routledge.

Feagin, J. R., & Cobas, J. A. (2013). *Latinos facing racism: Discrimination, resistance, and endurance.* Boulder, CO: Paradigm.

Feagin, J. R., Vera, H., & Imani, N. (1996). *The agony of education: Black students at White colleges and universities.* New York, NY: Routledge.

Fisher v. University of Texas at Austin, 133 U.S. 2411 (2013).

Friedel, J. N., Thornton, Z. M., D'Amico, M. M., & Kantsinas, S. G. (2013). *Performance-based funding: The national landscape.* Tuscaloosa: The University of Alabama, Education Policy Center.

Fries-Britt, S., & Turner, B. (2001). Facing stereotypes: A case study of Black students on a White campus. *Journal of College Student Development, 42,* 420–429.

Garces, L. M., & Mickey-Pabello, D. (2015). Racial diversity in the medical profession: The impact of affirmative action bans on underrepresented student of color matriculation in medical schools. *The Journal of Higher Education, 86*(2), 264–294.

Garcia, R. (1995). Critical race theory and Proposition 187: The racial politics of immigration law. *Chicano-Latino Law Review, 17,* 118–148.

Garrison-Wade, D., Diggs, G., Estrada, D., & Galindo, R. (2012). Lift every voice and sing: Faculty of color face the challenges of the tenure track. *Urban Review, 44,* 90–112.

Gartner, S. L., & Dovidio, J. F. (1986). The aversive form of racism. In J. F. Dovidio & S. L. Gaertner (Eds.), *Prejudice, discrimination, and racism* (pp. 61–89). Orlando, FL: Academic Press.

Gasman, M. (2008). *Envisioning Black colleges: A history of the United Negro College Fund.* Baltimore: Johns Hopkins University Press.

Gee, H. (1999). Beyond Black and White: Selected writings by Asian Americans within the Critical Race Theory Movement. *St. Mary's Law Journal, 30*(3), 759–799.

Gil, D. G. (1998). *Confronting injustice and oppression: Concepts and strategies for social workers.* New York: Columbia University Press.

Gildersleeve, R. E., Croom, N. N., & Vasquez, P. L. (2011). "Am I going crazy?!": A critical race analysis of doctoral education. *Equity & Excellence in Education, 44*(1), 93–114.

Gillborn, D. (2005). Education policy as an act of white supremacy: Whiteness, critical racetheory, and education reform. *Journal of Education Policy, 20*(4), 485–505.

Giroux, H.A. (2010). Bare pedagogy and the scourge of neoliberalism: Rethinking higher education as a democratic public sphere. *The Educational Forum, 74*(3), 184–196.

Gonzalez, K. P. (2003). Campus culture and the experiences of Chicano students in a predominantly White university. *Urban Education, 37*(2), 193–218.

Gordon, L., & Rojas, R. (2011, March 19). UCLA won't discipline creator of controversial video, who later withdraws from university. *Los Angeles Times.* Retrieved from http://articles.latimes.com/2011/mar/19/local/la-me-ucla-speech-20110319

Gould, S. J. (1996). *The mismeasure of man.* New York: W. W. Norton.

Gratz v. Bollinger et al., 539 U.S. 244 (2003).

Griffin, R., Ward, L., & Phillips, A. (2014). Still flies in buttermilk: Black male faculty, critical race theory, and composite counterstorytelling. *International Journal of Qualitative Studies in Education, 27*(10), 1354–1375.

Grutter v. Bollinger et al., 539 U.S. 203 (2003).

Gusa, D. L. (2010). White institutional presence: The impact of whiteness on campus climate. *Harvard Educational Review, 80*(4), 464–490.

Hamermesh, D., & Parker, M. (2005). Beauty in the classroom: Instructors' pulchritude and putative pedagogical productivity. *Economics of Education Review, 24*(4), 369–376.

Haney López, I. (1996). *White by law: The legal construction of race.* New York, NY: New York University Press.

Harding, D. J. (2010). *For-profit colleges, educational attainment, and labor market outcomes.* Retrieved from http://www.psc.isr.umich.edu/research/project-detail/34723

Harper, S. R. (2009). Niggers no more: A critical race counternarrative on Black make student achievement at predominantly White colleges and universities. *International Journal of Qualitative Studies in Education, 22*(6), 697–712.

Harper, S. R. (2012). Race without racism: How higher education researchers minimize racist institutional norms. *The Review of Higher Education, 36*(1), 9–29.

Harper, S. R., & Hurtado, S. (2007). Nine themes in campus racial climates and implications for institutional transformation. In S. R. Harper & L. D. Patton (Eds.), *Responding to the realities of race on campus.* New Directions for Student Services (No. 120, pp. 7–24). San Francisco, CA: Jossey-Bass.

Harper, S. R., Patton, L. D., & Wooden, O. S. (2009). Access and equity for African American students in higher education: A critical race historical analysis of policy efforts. *The Journal of Higher Education, 80*(4), 389–414.

Harrell, S. P. (2000). A multidimensional conceptualization of racism-related stress: Implications for the well-being of people of color. *American Journal of Orthopsychiatry, 70*(1), 42–57.

Harris, A. P. (2003). Race and essentialism in feminist legal theory. In A. K. Wing (Ed.), *Critical Race feminism: A reader* (2nd ed., pp. 34–41). New York, NY: New York University Press.

Harris, C. I. (1993). Whiteness as property. *Harvard Law Review, 106*(8), 1707–1791.

Harris, F., & Bensimon, E. M. (2007). The equity scorecard: A collaborative approach to assess and respond to racial/ethnic disparities in student outcomes. *New Directions for Student Services*, No. *120*, 77–84.

Heller, D. E. (2006). The impact of student loans on college access. In S. Baum, M. McPherson, & P. Steele (Eds.). *The effectiveness of student aid policies: What the research tells us* (pp. 39–68). New York: Lumina Foundation for Education.

Hentschke, G. C., Lechuga, V. M., & Tierney, W. G. (2010). *For-profit colleges and universities: Their markets, regulation, performance, and place in higher education.* Sterling, VA: Stylus.

Hillman, N. W. (2013). Economic diversity in elite higher education: Do no-loan programs impact Pell enrollments?. *The Journal of Higher Education, 84*(6), 806–833.

Hiltzik, M. (2014, September 15). The Salaita case and the big money takeover of state universities. *Los Angeles Times.* Retrieved from http://www.latimes.com/business/hiltzik/la-fi-mh-the-salaita-case-20140915-column.html

Hoffman, A. (1974). *Unwanted Mexican Americans in the great depression: Repatriation pressures, 1929–1939.* Tuscon: University of Arizona Press.

Ho'omanawanui, K. (2004). Hā, mana, leo (breath, spirit, voice): Kanaka Maoli empowerment through literature. *American Indian Quarterly, 28*(1–2), 86–91.

Huber, L. P. (2009). Challenging racist nativist framing: Acknowledging the community cultural wealth of undocumented Chicana college students to reframe the immigration debate. *Harvard Educational Review, 79*(4), 704–730.

Huber, L. P., & Malagon, M. C. (2006). Silenced struggles: The experiences of Latina and Latino undocumented college students in California. *Nevada Law Journal, 7*, 841.

Hune, S., & Chan, K. S. (1997). *Special focus: Asian Pacific American demographic and educational trends: Fifteenth annual status report.* Washington, DC: American Council on Education.

Hurtado, S. (1992). The campus racial climate: Contexts and conflict. *Journal of Higher Education, 63*(5), 539–569.

Hurtado, S., & Carter, D. (1997). Effects of college transition and perceptions of the campus racial climate on Latina/o college students' sense of belonging. *Sociology of Education, 70*, 324–345.

Hurtado, S., Milem, J. F., Clayton-Pedersen, A. R., & Allen, W. (1998). Enhancing campus climates for racial/ethnic diversity: Educational policy and practice. *The Review of Higher Education, 21*(3), 279–302.

Hurtado, S., Milem, J. F., Clayton-Pedersen, A. R., & Allen, W. R. (1999). Enhancing campus climates for racial/ethnic diversity: Educational policy and practice. *Review of Higher Education, 21*(3).

Iloh, C., & Toldson, I. A. (2013). Black students in 21st century higher education: A closer look at for-profit and community colleges. *The Journal of Negro Education, 82*(3), 205–212.

Institute for Higher Education Policy (2002). *The policy of choice: expanding student options in higher education.* Washington, DC: Author.

Iverson, S. D. (2007). Camouflaging power and privilege: A critical race analysis of university diversity policies. *Education Administration Quarterly, 43*(5), 586–611.

Jackson, J. F. L., & O'Callaghan, E. M. (2009). Ethnic and racial administrative diversity: Understanding work life realities and experiences in higher education. *ASHE Higher Education Report, 32*(3). San Francisco: Jossey-Bass.

Jackson, R. L., & Crawley, A. (2003). White student confessions about a Black male professor: A cultural contracts theory approach to intimate conversations about race and worldview. *The Journal of Men's Studies, 12*(1), 25–41.

Jayakumar, U. M. (2008). Can higher education meet the needs of an increasingly diverse and global society? Campus diversity and cross-cultural workforce competencies. *Harvard Educational Review, 78*(4), 615–651.

Jayakumar, U. M., & Adamian, A. S. (2015). Toward a critical race praxis for educational research: Lessons from affirmative action and social science advocacy. *Journal Committed to Social Change on Race and Ethnicity, 1*(1), 22–58.

Jayakumar, U. M., Howard, T. C., Allen, W. R., & Han, J. C. (2009). Racial privilege in the professoriate: An exploration of campus climate, retention, and satisfaction. *Journal of Higher Education, 80*(5), 538–563.

Jayakumar, U. M., & Museus, S. D. (2012). Mapping the intersection of campus cultures and equitable outcomes among racially diverse student populations. In S. D. Museus & U. M. Jayakumar (Eds.), *Creating campus cultures: Fostering success among racially diverse student populations* (pp. 1–27). New York: Routledge.

Jencks, C., & Phillips, M. (2011). *The Black-White test score gap.* Washington, DC: Brookings Institution Press.

Johnson, K. (1997). Racial hierarchy, Asian Americans and Latinos as "foreigners," and social change: Is law the way to go? *Oregon Law Review, 76*, 347–368.

Jones, J. M. (1997). *Prejudice and Racism* (2nd ed.). New York, NY: McGraw-Hill.

Jones, T. (2014). *Performance funding at MSIs: Considerations and possible measures for public minority-serving institutions.* Atlanta, GA: Southern Education Foundation.

Kame'eleihiwa, L. (1992). *Native land and foreign desires: Pehea la e pono ai?* Honolulu, HI: Bishop Museum Press.

Karabel, J. (2005). *The chosen: The hidden history of admission at Harvard, Yale, and Princeton.* New York, NY: Houghton Mifflin.

Katznelson, I. (2005). *When affirmative action was white: An untold story of racial inequality in the twentieth century.* New York: W.W. Norton & Company.

Kellner, D. (2000). Globalization and new social movements: Lessons for critical theory and pedagogy. In N. Burbules & C. Torres (Eds.), *Globalization and education* (pp. 312–330). New York, NY: Routledge.

Kezar, A. J. (2012). Shared leadership for creating campus cultures that support students of color. In S. D. Museus & U. M. Jayakumar (Eds.), *Creating campus cultures: Fostering success among racially diverse student populations* (pp. 150–167). New York, NY: Routledge.

Kim, Y. K., Chang, M. J., & Park, J. J. (2009). Engaging with faculty: Examining rates, predictors, and educational effects for Asian American undergraduates. *Journal of Diversity in Higher Education, 2*(4), 206–218.

Kotori, C., & Malaney, G. D. (2003). Asian American students' perceptions of racism, reporting behaviors, and awareness of legal rights and procedures. *NASPA Journal, 40*(3), 56–76.

Kuh, G. D. (2005). Getting off the dime. In *Exploring different dimensions of student engagement: 2005 annual report.* Bloomington, IN: Center for Postsecondary Research.

Kuh, G. D., & Love, P. G. (2000). A cultural perspective on student departure. In J. M. Braxton (Ed.), *Reworking the student departure puzzle* (pp. 196–212). Nashville, TN: Vanderbilt University Press.

Labaree, D.F. (1997). Public goods, private goods: The American struggle over educational goals. *American Educational Research Journal, 34*(1), 39–81.

Ladson-Billings, G. (2009). Just what is critical race theory and what's it doing in a nice field like education? In E. Taylor, D. Gillborn, & G. Ladson-Billings (Eds.), *Foundations of critical race theory in education* (pp. 17–35). New York, NY: Routledge.

Ladson-Billings, G., & Tate, W. F. (1995). Toward a Critical Race theory of education. *Teachers College Record, 97*(1), 47–68.

Lawrence, C. R. (1995). The word and the river: Pedagogy as scholarship, as struggle. In K. Crenshaw, N. Gotanda, G. Peller, & K. Thomas (Eds.), *Critical race theory: The key writings that formed the movement* (pp. 336–356). New York, NY: The New Press.

Ledesma, M. C., & Calderon, D. (2015). Critical race theory in education: A review of past literature and a look to the future. *Qualitative Inquiry, 21*(3), 206–222.

Ledesma, M. C., & Solórzano, D. (2013). Naming their pain: How everyday racial micro aggressions impact students and teachers. In D. J. Carter & F. Tuitt (Eds.), *Contesting the myth of a "post-racial" era: The continued significance of race in U.S. Education* (pp. 112–127). New York, NY: Peter Lang.

Lee, S. M. (2002). Do Asian American faculty face a glass ceiling in higher education? *American Educational Research Journal, 39*(3), 695–724.

Lee, S. (2012). The for-profit higher education industry, by the numbers. *Propublica.* Retrieved from http://www.propublica.org/article/the-for-profit-higher-education-industry-bythe-numbers/

Lemann, N. (2000). *The big test: The secret history of the American meritocracy*. New York, NY: Farrar, Straus, Giroux.

Levin, J. S., Walker, L., Jackson-Boothby, J., & Haberler, Z. (2013). *Community colleges and their faculty of color: Matching teachers and students*. Riverside, CA: California Community College Collaborative.

Lewis, A. E., Chesler, M., & Forman, T. A. (2000). The impact of "colorblind" ideologies on students of color: Intergroup relations at a predominantly White university. *The Journal of Negro Education*, *69*(1/2), 74–91.

Liu, A. (2009). Critical race theory, Asian Americans, and higher education: A review of research. *InterActions: UCLA Journal of Education and Information Studies*, *5*(2), 1–12.

Locks, A. M., Hurtado, S., Bowman, N. A., & Oseguera, L. (2008). Extending notions of campus climate and diversity to students' transition to college. *The Review of Higher Education*, *31*(3), 257–285.

Lomawaima, K. T., & McCarty, T. L. (2006). *"To remain an Indian": Lessons in democracy from a century of Native American education*. New York, NY: Teachers College Press.

Long, B. T. & Riley, E. (2007). Financial aid: A broken bridge to college access?. *Harvard Educational Review*, *77*(1), 39–63.

López, I. H. (2014). *Dog whistle politics: How coded racial appeals have reinvented racism & wrecked the middle class*. New York: Oxford.

Lowen, J. (1996). *Lies my teacher told me: Everything your American history textbook got wrong*. New York, NY: Touchstone.

Matsuda, M. J. (1996). *Where is your body? Essays on race, gender and the law*. Boston: Beacon Press.

Matsuda, M. J., Lawrence, C. R., III, Delgado, R., & Crenshaw, K. W. (1993). *Words that wound: Critical race theory, assaultive speech, and the first amendment*. Boulder, CO: Westview Press.

McCormick, A., & Kinzie, J. (2014). Refocusing the quality discourse: The United States National Survey of Student Engagement. In H. Coates (Ed.), *Engaging university students: International insights from system-wide studies*. New York, NY: Springer.

McCoy, D. L., & Rodricks, D. J. (2015). Critical Race Theory in higher education: 20 years of theoretical and research innovations. *ASHE Higher Education Report*, *41*(3). San Francisco, CA: Jossey-Bass.

Meyer, M. A. (2008). Indigenous and authentic: Hawaiian epistemology and the triangulation of meaning. In N. K. Denzin, Y. S. Lincoln, & L. T. Smith (Eds.), *Handbook of critical and indigenous methodologies* (pp. 217–232). Los Angeles, CA: SAGE.

Muñoz, F. M. (2009). Critical race theory and the landscapes of higher education. *The Vermont Connection*, *30*, 53–62.

Museus, S. D. (2007). Using qualitative methods to assess diverse institutional cultures. In S. R. Harper & S. D. Museus (Eds.), *Using qualitative methods in institutional assessment*. New Directions for Institutional Research (No. 136, pp. 29–40). San Francisco, CA: Jossey-Bass.

Museus, S. D. (2008). The model minority and the inferior minority myths: Understanding stereotypes and their implications for student involvement. *About Campus*, *13*(3), 2–8.

Museus, S. D. (2011). Generating Ethnic Minority Success (GEMS): A collective-cross case analysis of high-performing colleges. *Journal of Diversity in Higher Education*, *4*(3), 147–162.

Museus, S. D. (2013a). Asian Americans and Pacific Islanders: A national portrait of growth, diversity, and inequality. In S. D. Museus, D. C. Maramba, & R. T. Teranishi (Eds.), *The misrepresented minority: New insights on Asian Americans and Pacific Islanders, and the implications for higher education*. Sterling, VA: Stylus.

Museus, S. D. (2013b). *Asian American students in higher education*. New York, NY: Routledge.

Museus, S. D. (2014). The Culturally Engaging Campus Environments (CECE) model: A new theory of college success among racially diverse student populations. In *Higher Education: Handbook of Theory and Research*. New York, NY: Springer.

Museus, S. D. (2015). *The CECE Model and Indicators*. Denver, CO: CECE Project.

Museus, S. D., & Harris, F., III. (2010). Success among college students of color: How institutional culture matters. In T. E. Dancy II (Ed.), *Managing diversity: (Re)visioning equity on college campuses* (pp. 25–44). New York, NY: Peter Lang.

Museus, S. D., & Iftikar, J. (2014). *Asian Critical Theory (AsianCrit)*. In M. Y. Danico & J. G. Golson (Eds.), *Asian American Society*. Thousand Oaks, CA: Sage Publications and Association for Asian American Studies.

Museus, S. D., Jayakumar, U. M., & Robinson, T. (2012). Effects of racial representation on the persistence of community college students: An examination of conditional and indirect effects. *Journal of College Student Retention: Theory, Research, and Practice, 13*(4), 549–572.

Museus, S. D., & Kiang, P. N. (2009). The model minority myth and how it contributes to the invisible minority reality in higher education research. In S. D. Museus (Ed.), *Conducting research on Asian Americans in higher education*. New Directions for Institutional Research (No. 142, pp. 5–15). San Francisco, CA: Jossey-Bass.

Museus, S. D., Nichols, A. H., & Lambert, A. (2008). Racial differences in the effects of campus racial climate on degree completion: A structural model. *The Review of Higher Education, 32*(1), 107–134.

Museus, S. D., & Park, J. J. (2015). The continuing significances of racism in the lives of Asian American college students. *Journal of College Student Development, 56*(6), 551–569.

Museus, S. D., & Quaye, S. J. (2009). Toward an intercultural perspective of racial and ethnic minority college student persistence. *The Review of Higher Education, 33*(1), 67–94.

Museus, S. D., Ravello, J. N., & Vega, B. E. (2012). The campus racial culture: A critical race counterstory. In S. D. Museus & U. M. Jayakumar (Eds.), *Creating campus cultures: Fostering success among racially diverse student populations* (pp. 28–45). New York, NY: Routledge.

Museus, S. D., & Saelua, N. (2014). The power of intersectionality in higher education research: The case of Asian Americans and Pacific Islanders in higher education. In D. Mitchell Jr. (Eds.), *Intersectionality and higher education: Theory, research, and practice* (pp. 68–77). New York, NY: Peter Lang.

Museus, S. D., & Truong, K. A. (2013). Racism and sexism in cyberspace: Engaging stereotypes of Asian American women and men to facilitate student learning and development. *About Campus, 18*(4), 14–21.

National Center for Education Statistics [NCES] (2013). *Race/ethnicity of college faculty*. Washington, DC: Author.

National Center for Higher Education Management Systems (2013). *Outcomes-based funding: The wave of implementation*. Boulder, CO: Author.

Neville K., & Parker, T. L. (2014, November). *The influence of students' racial and ethnic identity development on their perceptions of African American faculty*. Paper presented at the Association for the Study of Higher Education Annual Meeting, Washington, DC.

Ngo, B., & Lee, S. (2007). Complicating the image of model minority success: A review of Southeast Asian American education. *Review of Educational Research, 77*(4), 415–453.

Northwestern University (2014). *Report of the John Evans Study Committee*. Evanston, IL: Northwestern University.

Oakes, J. (2005). *Keeping track*. New Haven, CT: Yale University Press.

Oakes, J., Rogers, J., Lipton, M., & Morrell, E. (2002). The social construction of college access Confronting the technical, cultural, and political barriers to low-income students of color. In W. G. Tierney & L. S. Haggedorn (Eds.), *Increasing access to college: Extending possibilities for all students* (pp. 105–121). Albany: State University of New York Press.

Omi, M., & Winant, H. (1994). *Racial formation in the United States: From the 1960s to the 1990s*. New York, NY: Routledge.

Omi, M., & Winant, H. (2015). *Racial formation in the United States* (3rd ed.). New York, NY: Routledge.

Oliff, P., Palacios, V., Johnson, I., & Leachman, M. (2013, March 19). Recent deep state higher education cuts may harm students and the economy for years to come. In *Center on Budget and Policy Priorities*. Retrieved from http://www.cbpp.org/cms/index .cfm?fa=view&id=3927#_ftn11

Padilla, A. M. (1994). Ethnic minority scholars, research, and mentoring: Current and future issues. *Educational Researcher, 23*(4), 24–27.

Padilla, R. V., & Chavez Chavez, R. (1995). *The leaning ivory tower: Latino professors in American universities*. Albany: State University of New York Press.

Palepu, A., Carr, P. L., Friedman, R. H., Amos, H., Ash, A. S., & Moskowitz, M. A. (1995). Minority faculty and academic rank in medicine. *Journal of the American Medical Association, 250*, 767–771.

Park, J. J. (2008). Race and the Greek system in the 21st century: Centering the voices of Asian American women. *The NASPA Journal, 45*(1), 103–132.

Parker, L., & Lynn, M. (2002). What's race got to do with it? Critical race theory's conflicts with and connections to qualitative research methodology and epistemology. *Qualitative Inquiry, 8*(1), 7–22.

Patton, L. D., & Catching, C. (2009). "Teaching while Black": Narratives of African American student affairs faculty. *International Journal of Qualitative Studies in Education, 22*(6), 713–728.

Patton, T. O. (2004). Reflections of a Black woman professor: Racism and sexism in academia. *Howard Journal of Communications, 15*(3), 185–200.

Perry, G., Moore, H., Edwards, C., Acosta, K., & Frey, C. (2009). Maintaining credibility and authority as an instructor of color in diversity-education classrooms: A qualitative inquiry. *Journal of Higher Education, 80*(1), 80–105.

Pike, G. R., & Kuh, G. D. (2006). Relationships among structural diversity, informal peer interactions and perceptions of the campus environment. *The Review of Higher Education, 29*(4), 425–450.

Pittman, C. (2010). Race and gender oppression in the classroom: The experiences of women faculty of color with white male students. *Teaching Sociology, 38*(3), 183–196.

Poloma, A. (2014). Why teaching faculty diversity (still) matters. *Peabody Journal of Education, 89*, 336–346.

Prucha, F. P. (1995). *The great father: The United States government and the American Indians*. Lincoln: University of Nebraska Press.

Regents of the University of California v. Bakke, 438 U.S. 265 (1978).

Resmovits, J. (2014, June 24). Fisher v. University of Texas at Austin ruling leaves universities in limbo. *Huffpost Politics*. Retrieved from http://www.huffingtonpost.com/2013/06/24/fisher-v-university-of-texas-at-austin-ruling_n_3434687.html

Reyes, N. A. S. (2014). *A space for survivance: Locating Kānaka Maoli through the resonance and dissonance of Critical Race Theory*. Paper presented at the 2014 meeting of the Association for the Study of Higher Education, Washington, DC.

Rich, M. (2014, March 21). School data finds pattern of any quality along racial lines. *New York Times*.

Robie, D. (1990). *Blood on their banner: Nationalist struggles in the South Pacific*. Atlantic Highlands, NJ: Zed.

Romell, R. (2012). 7 killed, including shooter, at Sikh Temple in Oak Creek. *Journal Sentinel*. Retrieved from http://www.jsonline.com/news/crime/reports-of-people-shot-at-sikh-temple-in-oak-creek-qc6cgc0-165059506.html

Russell, M. (1992). Entering great America: Reflections on race and the convergence of progressive legal theory and practice. *Hastings Law Journal, 43*, 749–767.

Saito, N. T. (1997). Alien and non-alien alike: Citizenship, "foreignness," and racial hierarchy in American law. *Oregon Law Review, 76*, 261–345.

Sander, R., & Taylor, S. (2012). *Mismatch: How affirmative action hurts students it's intended to help, and why universities won't admit it*. New York, NY: Basic Books.

Satcher, D., Fryer, G. E., McCann, J., Troutman, A., Woolf, S. H., & Rust, G. (2005). What if we were equal? A comparison of the black-white mortality gap in 1960 and 2000. *Health Affairs, 24*(2), 459–464.

Schuette v. Coalition to Defend Affirmative Action, 572 U.S. __ (2014).

Sears, D. O. (1988). Symbolic racism. In P. A. Katz & D. A. Taylor (Eds.), *Eliminating racism: Profiles in controversy* (pp. 53–84). New York, NY: Plenum Press.

Selmi, M. (1997). Public vs. private enforcement of civil rights: The case of housing and employment. *UCLA Law Review, 45*, 1401–1459.

Sgueglia, K., Marcellino, M., & Sanchez, R. (2014, September 2). From NY to Texas, KKK recruits with candies and fliers. *CNN*. Retrieved from http://www.cnn.com/2014/08/31/us/new-york-kkk-recruitment/

Skrentny, J. D. (1996). *The ironies of affirmative action: Politics, culture, and justice in America*. Chicago: University of Chicago Press.

Smedley, B. D., Myers, H. F., & Harrell, S. P. (1993). Minority-status stresses and the college adjustment of ethnic minority freshmen. *Journal of Higher Education, 64*(4), 434–452.

Smith, D. G. (2011). *Diversity's promise for higher education: Making it work*. Baltimore, MD: Johns Hopkins University Press.

Smith, D. G. (2015). *Diversity's promise for higher education: Making it work* (Second edition). Baltimore, MD: Johns Hopkins University Press.

Smith, W. A. (2004). Black faculty coping with racial battle fatigue: The campus racial climate in a post-civil rights era. In D. Cleveland (Ed.), *A long way to go: Conversations about race by African American faculty and graduate students* (pp. 171–190). New York, NY: Peter Lang.

Smith, W. A., Allen, W. R., & Danley, L. L. (2007). "Assume the position ... you fit the description": Psychosocial experiences and racial battle fatigue among African American male college students. *American Behavioral Scientist, 51*(4), 551–578.

Snyder, T., & Dillow, S. (2012). *Digest of education statistics, 2011.* Retrieved from http://nces.ed.gov/pubs2012/2012001.pdf

Solórzano, D. G. (1997). Images and words that wound: Critical race theory, racial stereotyping, and teacher education. *Teacher Education Quarterly,* 5–19.

Solórzano, D. G. (1998). Critical race theory, race and gender microaggressions, and the experience of Chicana and Chicano scholars. *International Journal of Qualitative Studies in Education, 11*(1), 121–136.

Solórzano, D. G., Ceja, M., & Yosso, T. (2000). Critical race theory, racial microaggressions, and campus racial climate: The experiences of African American college students. *Journal of Negro Education,* 60–73.

Solórzano, D. G., & Delgado Bernal, D. (2001). Examining transformational resistance through a critical race and LatCrit theory framework Chicana and Chicano students in an urban context. *Urban Education, 36*(3), 308–342.

Solórzano, D. G., & Ornelas, A. (2002). A critical race analysis of advanced placement classes: A case of educational inequality. *Journal of Latinos and Education, 1*(4), 215–229.

Solórzano, D. G., & Ornelas, A. (2004). A critical race analysis of Latina/o and African American advanced placement enrollment in public high schools. *The High School Journal, 87*(3), 15–26.

Solórzano, D. G., & Yosso, T. J. (2001). Critical race and LatCrit theory and method: Counter-storytelling. *International Journal of Qualitative Studies in Education, 14*(4), 471–495.

St. John, E. P., Duan-Barnett, N., & Moronski-Chapman, K. M. (2013). *Public policy and higher education: Reframing strategies for preparation, access, and college success.* New York: Routledge.

Stanley, C. A. (2006). Coloring the academic landscape: Faculty of color breaking the silence in predominantly White colleges and universities. *American Educational Research Journal, 43,* 701–736.

Stanley, C. (2007). When counter narratives meet master narrative in the journal editorial-review process. *Educational Researcher, 36*(1), 14–24.

Steele, C. (1999). A threat in the air: How stereotypes shape intellectual identity and performance. *American Psychologist, 52*(6), 613–629.

Steele, C. M., & Aronson, J. (1995). Stereotype threat and the intellectual test performance of African Americans. *Journal of personality and social psychology, 69*(5), 797–811.

Sue, D. W. (2003). Cultural competence in the treatment of ethnic minority populations. In D. W. Sue (Ed.), *Psychological treatment of ethnic minority populations.* Washington DC: APA Press.

Sue, D. W., Bucceri, J., Lin, A. I., Nadal, K. L., & Torino, G. C. (2007). Racial microaggressions and the Asian American experience. *Cultural Diversity and Ethnic Minority Psychology, 13*(1), 72–81.

Sue, D. W., Capodilupo, C. M., & Holder, A. M. B. (2008). Racial microaggressions in the life experience of Black Americans. *Professional Psychology: Research and Practice, 39*(3), 329–336.

Sue, D. W., Capodilupo, C. M., Torino, G. C., Bucceri, J. M, Holder, A. M. B., Nadal, K. L., & Esquilin, M. (2007). Racial micro-aggressions in everyday life: Implications for clinical practice. *American Psychologist, 62*(4), 271–286.

Suzuki, B. H. (1977). Education and the socialization of Asian Americans: A revisionist analysis of the "model minority" thesis. *Amerasia Journal, 4*(2), 23–51.

Suzuki, B. H. (2002). Revisiting the model minority stereotype: Implications for student affairs practice and higher education. *Working with Asian American college students.* New Directions for Student Services (No. 97, pp. 21–32). San Francisco, CA: Jossey-Bass.

Takaki, R. (1989). *Strangers from a different shore: A history of Asian Americans* (Rev. ed.). Boston: Little, Brown.

Tamura, E. H. (2001a). Asian Americans in the history of education: An historiographical essay. *History of Education Quarterly, 41*(1), 58–71.

Tamura, E. H., (2001b). Introduction: Asian Americans and educational history. *History of Education Quarterly, 43*(1), 1–9.

Tate, W. F. (1997). Critical race theory and education: History, theory, and implications. *Review of Research in Education, 22,* 195–247.

Teranishi, R. T., Behringer, L. B., Grey, E. A., & Parker, T. L. (2009). Critical race theory and research on Asian Americans and Pacific Islanders in higher education. In S. D. Museus (Ed.), *Conducting research on Asian Americans in higher education.* New Directions for Institutional Research (No. 142, 57–68). San Francisco, CA: Jossey-Bass.

Thelin, J. R. (2011). *A history of American higher education.* Baltimore, MD: John Hopkins University Press.

The Pew Charitable Trusts. (2015). *Federal and state funding of higher education: A changing landscape.* Washington, DC: Author.

Thernstrom, S., & Thernstrom, A. (1997). *America in black and white: One nation, indivisible.* New York, NY: Touchstone.

Thompson, K. (2010, June 30). Arrest of Harvard's Henry Louis Gates Jr. was avoidable, report says. *The Washington Post.* Retrieved from http://www.washingtonpost.com/wp-dyn/content/article/2010/06/30/AR2010063001356.html

Tierney, W. G. (1992). An anthropological analysis of student participation in college. *Journal of Higher Education, 63*(6), 603–618.

Tierney, W. G. (1999). Models of minority college-going and retention: Cultural integrity versus cultural suicide. *The Journal of Negro Education, 68*(1), 80–91.

Tierney, W. G., & Sallee, M. W. (2008). Do organizational structures and strategies increase faculty diversity? A cultural analysis. *American Academic, 4*(1), 159–184.

Tinker, G. E. (1993). *Missionary conquest: The gospel and Native American cultural genocide.* Bolingbrook, IL: Augsburg Fortress.

Tinsley-Jones, H. (2003). Racism: Calling a spade a spade. *Psychotherapy: Theory, Research, Practice, Training, 40,* 179–186.

Tinto, V. (1987). *Leaving college: Rethinking the causes and cures of student attrition.* Chicago: University of Chicago Press.

Trask, H. K. (2000). Settlers of color and "immigrant" hegemony: "Locals" in Hawai'i. *Amerasia Journal, 26*(2), 1–24.

Trower, C. A. (2003). Leveling the field. *The Academic Workplace, 14*(2), 1, 3, 6–7, 14–15.

Trower, C. A., & Chait, R. P. (2002). Faculty diversity: Too little for too long. *Harvard Magazine, 104*(4), 33–37.

Truong, K. A., & Museus, S. D. (2012). Responding to racism and racial trauma in doctoral study: An inventory for coping and mediating relationships. *Harvard Educational Review, 82*(2), 226–254.

Truong, K. A., Museus, S. D., & McGuire, K. (2015). Vicarious racism: a qualitative analysis of experiences with secondhand racism in graduate education. *International Journal of Qualitative Studies in Education*.

Tuitt, F., Hanna, M., Martinez, L., Salazar, M., & Griffin, R. (2009). Teaching in the line of fire: Faculty of color in the academy. *Thought and Action, 65*, 65–74.

Turner, C. S. V. (1994). Guests in someone else's house: Students of color. *The Review of Higher Education, 17*(4), 355–370.

Turner, C. (2002). Women of color in academe: Living with multiple marginality. *Journal of Higher Education, 73*, 74–93.

Turner, C. S. V. (2003). Incorporation and marginalization in the academy: From border toward center for faculty of color? *Journal of Black Studies, 34*, 112–125.

Turner, C. S. V., Garcia, M., Nora, A., & Rendon, L. I. (Eds.). (1996). *Racial & ethnic diversity in higher education*. Needham Heights, MA: Simon & Schuster Custom.

Turner, C. S. V., Gonzalez, J. C., & Wood, J. L. (2008). Faculty of color in academe: What 20 years of literature tells us. *Journal of Diversity in Higher Education, 1*(3), 139–168.

Turner, C., Myers, S., & Creswell, J. (1999). Exploring underrepresentation: The case of faculty of color in the Midwest. *Journal of Higher Education, 70*(1), 27–59.

Umemoto, K. (1989). "On strike!" San Francisco State College strike, 1968–69: The role of Asian American students. *Amerasia Journal, 15*(1), 3–41.

U.S. Bureau of Labor Statistics (2014). *Labor force statistics from the current population survey*. Washington, DC: Author.

U.S. Census Bureau (2010). *America's families and living arrangements: 2010*. Washington, DC: Author.

U.S. Census Bureau (2012). *2012 population projections*. Washington, DC: Author.

Valencia, R. R. (1997). Conceptualizing the notion of deficit thinking. In R. R. Valencia (Ed.), *The evolution of deficit thinking: Educational thought and practice*. Washington, DC: The Falmer Press.

Valencia, R. R. (2008). *Chicano students and the courts: The Mexican American legal struggle for educational equality*. New York, NY: New York University Press.

Vargas, L. (Ed.). (2002). *Women faculty of color in the White classroom: Narratives on the pedagogical implications of teacher diversity*. New York, NY: Peter Lang.

Villalpando, O. (2003). Self-segregation or self-preservation? A critical race theory and Latina/o critical theory analysis of a study of Chicana/o college students. *Qualitative Studies in Education, 16*(5), 619–646.

Villalpando, O. (2004). Practical considerations of critical race theory and Latino critical theory for Latino college students. In A. M. Ortiz (Ed.), *Addressing the unique needs of Latino American students*. New Directions for Student Services (No. 105, 41–50). San Francisco, CA: Jossey-Bass.

Vizenor, G. (Ed.). (2008). *Survivance: Narratives of Native Presence*. Lincoln: University of Nebraska Press.

Vizenor, G., & Lee, A. R. (1999). *Postindian conversations*. Lincoln: University of Nebraska Press.

Wijeyesinghe, C. L., Griffin, P., & Love, B. (1997). Racism curriculum design. In M. Adams, L. A. Bell, & P. Griffin (Eds.), *Teaching for diversity and social justice* (pp. 82–110). New York, NY: Routledge.

Wilder, C. S. (2013). *Ebony & ivy: Race, slavery, and the troubled history of American universities*. New York, NY: Bloomsbury Press.

Winant, H. (2011). Review of the book *The problem of the future world: W. E. B. Du Bois and the race concept at midcentury*, by E. Porter. *Ethnic and Racial Studies 34*(11), 1995–2007.

Witham, K. A., & Bensimon, E. M. (2012). Creating a culture of inquiry and equity around student success. In S. D. Museus & U. M. Jayakumar (Eds.), *Creating campus cultures: Fostering success among racially diverse student populations* (pp. 46–67). New York, NY: Routledge.

Wood, F. (1968). *Black scare: The racist response to emancipation and reconstruction*. Los Angeles: University of California Press.

Wright, E. K., & Balutski, B. J. N. (2013). The role of context, critical theory, and counternarratives in understanding Indigenous Pacific Islander identities and experiences. In S. D. Museus, D. C. Maramba, & R. T. Teranishi (Eds.), *The misrepresented minority: New insights on Asian Americans and Pacific Islanders, and their implications for higher education* (pp. 163–184). Sterling, VA: Stylus.

Wu, F. H. (1995). Neither black nor white: Asian Americans and affirmative action. *BC Third World LJ, 15*, 225.

Yan, W., & Museus, S. D. (2013). Asian American and Pacific Islander faculty and the glass ceiling in higher education. In S. D. Museus, D. C. Maramba, & R. T. Teranishi (Eds.), *The misrepresented minority: New insights on Asian Americans and Pacific Islanders, and the implications for higher education* (pp. 249–265). Sterling, VA: Stylus.

Yosso, T. J. (2005). Whose culture has capital? A critical race theory discussion of community cultural wealth. *Race Ethnicity and Education, 8*(1), 69–91.

Yosso, T. J., Parker, L., Solórzano, D. G., & Lynn, M. (2004). From Jim Crow to affirmative action and back again: A critical race discussion of racialized relationales and access to higher education. *Review of Research in Education, 28*, 1–25.

Yu, T. (2006). Challenging the politics of the "model minority" stereotype: A case for educational equity. *Equity & Excellence in Education, 39*, 325–333.

Zia, H. (2001). *Asian American dreams: The emergence of an American people*. New York, NY: Farrar, Straus and Giroux.

Zinn, H. (2005). *A people's history of the United States*. New York, NY: Harper Perennial Modern Classics.

Name Index

A

Acosta, K., 63, 64
Acuña, R. F., 41
Adamian, A. S., 55
Aguirre, A., 66
Alberts, H. C., 64, 65
Allen, W. R., 16, 27, 29, 30, 67
Amos, H., 62
Ancis, J. R., 67, 68
Ansley, F. L., 86
Antonio, A. L., 69
Aronson, J., 54
Ash, A. S., 62
Astin, A. W., 11, 69
Atkinson, R. C., 53
Au, W., 53

B

Balutski, B. J. N., 22, 24
Banaji, M. R., 45
Banda, R. M., 25
Barrett, D., 2
Bauer, K., 30, 31
Behringer, L. B., 22
Bell, D. A., 18, 19, 43
Benjamin, L., 66
Bensimon, E. M., 16, 34, 35, 75, 79
Better, S., 84
Bidwell, A., 54
Blaut, J. M., 42
Bodenhausen, G. V., 68
Bok, D., 5, 59

Bonilla-Silva, E., 4, 44–47
Bonner, F. A., 25
Bossman, J., 2
Bowen, W., 5
Bowman, N. A., 30
Brack, M. B., 41
Brayboy, B. M. J., 16, 21, 22, 24, 28
Brooks, D., 46
Brown, D., 11, 26
Brown-Nagin, T., 25, 26, 69
Brubacher, J. S., 11, 51
Bucceri, J., 22, 45
Bucceri, J. M., 45
Buenavista, T. L., 22, 69
Burnham, L. B., 1

C

Cabrera, N. L., 68
Calderon, D., 19
Calmore, J., 19
Capodilupo, C. M., 45
Carcamo, C., 1
Carey, K., 7, 10
Carmen, F., 61
Carr, P. L., 62
Carrigan, W. D., 41
Carter, D., 30
Carter Andrews, D. J., 26
Castagno, A. E., 22
Catching, C., 27, 63
Ceja, M., 25, 27, 30
Chait, R. P., 62

Chan, K. S., 66
Chan, S., 22, 40, 42
Chang, J. C., 31
Chang, M. J., 19, 20, 31, 67, 68, 69
Chang, R. S., 22
Chavez Chavez, R., 67
Chen, A. C., 22, 69
Cheryan, S., 68
Chesler, M., 63, 64, 68, 70, 71
Chon, M., 22
Claudia, G., 60
Clayton-Pedersen, A. R., 16, 29, 30
Cobas, J. A., 41
Cohen, A. M., 11
Collier, M. J., 64
Correll, J., 69
Covarrubias, P. O., 22
Crawley, A., 64
Crenshaw, K. W., 18, 19, 22, 47
Cress, C. M., 67
Creswell, J., 62, 66
Croom, N. N., 27

D

D'Amico, M. M., 59
Danley, L. L., 27, 67
Darder, A., 19
Davey, M., 2
Delgado, R., 16, 18, 19, 41, 43, 47, 79
Delgado Bernal, D., 21, 27, 43, 65, 66
Deming, D., 60
Denson, D., 69
Denson, N., 69
DeVos, T., 45
Diggs, G., 67
Dill, D. D., 60
Dillow, S., 61
Dixson, A. D., 10, 19
Dovidio, J. F., 45
Dowd, A. C., 16, 34, 35, 75, 77
Duan-Barnett, N., 52, 57
Du Bois, W. E. B., 17
Dudley, M. K., 24
Duster, T., 69, 70

E

Edwards, C., 63, 64
Espino, M. M., 25
Espinoza, L., 20
Espiritu, Y. L., 22
Esquilin, M., 45
Estrada, D., 67

F

Feagin, J. R., 38, 40, 41, 67–69, 85
Forman, T. A., 68, 70, 71
Frey, C., 63, 64
Friedel, J. N., 59
Friedman, R. H., 62
Fries-Britt, S., 68
Fryer, G. E., 5

G

Gaertner, S. L., 45
Galindo, R., 67
Garces, L. M., 5
Garcia, M., 61
Garcia, R., 19
Garrison-Wade, D., 67
Gasman, M., 50
Gates, H. L., Jr., 1
Gee, H., 19, 20
Geiser, S., 53
Gil, D. G., 85
Gildersleeve, R. E., 27
Gillborn, D., 27
Giroux, H. A., 47
Gonzalez, J. C., 66
Gonzalez, K. P., 31, 69
Gotanda, N., 18, 19
Gould, S. J., 39, 53
Grey, E. A., 22
Griffin, P., 84
Griffin, R., 63
Guinier, L., 25, 26, 69
Gusa, D. L., 27

H

Haberler, Z., 61
Hakuta, K., 69
Hamermesh, D., 64

Han, J. C., 27
Haney López, I., 39
Hanna, M., 63
Harding, D. J., 60
Harper, S. R., 11, 12, 27, 50, 51, 75
Harrell, S. P., 13, 68, 85
Harris, A. P., 20
Harris, C. I., 19
Harris, F., 31, 35
Hazen, H. D., 64, 65
Heller, D. E., 58
Hentschke, G. C., 60
Hillman, N. W., 58
Hiltzik, M., 2
Hodson, G., 45
Hoffman, A., 41
Holder, A. M. B., 45
Ho'omanawanui, K., 24
Howard, T. C., 27
Huber, L. P., 20
Hughes, R. L., 25
Hune, S., 66
Hurtado, S., 16, 29, 30, 67, 75

I
Iftikar, J., 22, 24, 28
Ikeda, E. K., 67
Iloh, C., 60
Imani, N., 67–69
Iverson, S. D., 11, 26, 27

J
Jackson, J. F. L., 2, 61
Jackson, R. L., 64
Jackson-Boothby, J., 61
Jayakumar, U. M., 22, 27, 31, 55, 69, 79
Jencks, C., 52
Johnson, I., 57
Johnson, K., 20
Jones, J. M., 84
Jones, T., 59
Judd, C. M., 69

K
Kame'eleihiwa, L., 24, 42
Kantsinas, S. G., 59
Karabel, J., 11, 49, 53

Katz, L. F., 60
Katznelson, I., 51
Kawakami, K., 45
Kellner, D., 47
Kennedy, J. F., 56
Kenny, D. A., 69
Kezar, A. J., 34, 75, 79
Kiang, P. N., 22
Kim, D., 69
Kim, Y. K., 67, 68
Kinzie, J., 77
Kiyama, J. M., 25
Kotori, C., 67, 68
Kuh, G. D., 31, 67, 69

L
Labaree, D. F., 57
Ladson-Billings, G., 10, 19, 24, 47
Lambert, A., 29, 30
Lawrence, C. R., III, 18, 47
Leachman, M., 57
Lechuga, V. M., 60
Ledesma, M. C., 19, 27, 31
Lee, A. R., 24
Lee, S., 60, 68
Lee, S. J., 22
Lee, S. M., 62
Lemann, N., 53
Levin, J. S., 61
Levin, S., 69
Lewis, A. E., 68, 70, 71
Lin, A. I., 22, 45
Lipton, M., 53
Liu, A., 22
Locks, A. M., 30
Lomawaima, K. T., 40
Long, B. T., 58
López, H., 46
Love, B., 84
Love, P. G., 31
Lowen, J., 38
Lynn, M., 19, 20, 27

M
Malagon, M. C., 21
Malaney, G. D., 67

Malcolm, L., 35
Marbley, A. F., 25
Marcellino, M., 2
Martinez, L., 63
Martinez, R. O., 66
Matsuda, M. J., 18, 22, 47
McCann, J., 5
McCarty, T. L., 40
McCormick, A., 77
McCoy, D. L., 16, 19, 26, 28
McGruire, K. M., 85
Meyer, M. A., 24
Mickey-Pabello, D., 5
Milem, J. F., 16, 29, 30, 69
Misa, K., 69
Misa-Escalante, K., 22, 69
Mohr, J., 67, 68
Moore, H., 63, 64
Moronski-Chapman, K. M., 52, 57
Morrell, E., 53
Moskowitz, M. A., 62
Muñoz, F. M., 26
Muñoz, S. M., 25
Museus, S. D., 3, 10, 11, 16, 22, 24,
    27–32, 42, 55, 60 62, 67–71, 75–77, 85
Myers, H. F., 68
Myers, S., 62, 66
McGuire, K., 60

N
Nadal, K. L., 22, 45
Neville, K., 64
Ngo, B., 68
Nichols, A. H., 29, 30
Nora, A., 61

O
Oakes, J., 53
O'Callaghan, E. M., 61
Oliff, P., 57
Omi, M., 39, 40, 46, 85
Ornelas, A., 53
Oseguera, L., 30

P
Padilla, A. M., 66
Padilla, R. V., 67

Palacios, V., 57
Palepu, A., 62
Park, B., 69
Park, J. J., 67–71
Parker, L., 19, 20, 27
Parker, M., 64
Parker, T. L., 22, 64
Patton, L. D., 27, 50, 51, 63
Patton, T. O., 27
Peller, G., 18, 19
Perry, G., 63, 64
Phillips, A., 63
Phillips, M., 52
Pike, G. R., 69
Pittman, C., 65
Poloma, A., 61
Powell, R., 64
Prucha, F. P., 40

Q
Quaye, S. J., 31, 32, 70

R
Ravello, J. N., 27, 28, 31, 32, 81
Rendon, L. I., 61
Resmovits, J., 3
Reyes, N. A. S., 24, 25, 28
Rich, M., 6
Riley, E., 58
Robie, D., 42
Robinson, P. A., 25
Robinson, T., 28, 31, 55
Rodricks, D. J., 16, 19, 26, 28
Rogers, J., 53
Romell, R., 1
Rousseau, C. K., 10, 19
Rudy, W., 11, 51
Russell, M., 19
Rust, G., 5

S
Saelua, N., 22
Saenz, V., 69
Saito, N. T., 22
Salaita, S., 2
Salazar, M., 63

Sallee, M. W., 62
Sanchez, R., 2
Sander, R., 56
Satcher, D., 5
Sears, D. O., 45
Sedlacek, W. E., 67, 68
Selmi, M., 43
Sgueglia, K., 2
Skrentny, J. D., 51
Smedley, B. D., 68
Smith, D. G., 16, 34, 79, 80, 82
Smith, W. A., 27, 67
Snyder, T., 61
Solórzano, D. G., 16, 19–21, 24, 25, 27, 30, 53
St. John, E. P., 52, 57
Stanley, C. A., 12, 27, 63, 65, 66
Steele, C., 68
Steele, C. M., 54
Stefancic, J., 16, 18, 43, 47, 79
Sue, D. W., 22, 44, 45
Suzuki, B. H., 68

T
Takaki, R., 22, 40–42
Tamura, E. H., 42
Tate, W. F., 10, 18, 19, 26, 47
Taylor, S., 56
Teranishi, R. T., 22
Thelin, J. R., 11, 49–51
Theobald, R. B., 64, 65
Thernstrom, A., 56
Thernstrom, S., 56
Thomas, K., 18, 19
Thompson, K., 1
Thornton, Z. M., 59
Tierney, W. G., 31, 62
Tierney, W. G., 60
Tinker, G. E., 40
Tinsley-Jones, H., 45
Tinto, V., 11
Toldson, I. A., 60
Torino, G. C., 22, 45
Torres, G., 25, 26, 69
Torres, R. D., 19
Trask, H. K., 42

Troutman, A., 5
Trower, C. A., 62, 63
Truong, K. A., 3, 27, 60 68, 85
Tuitt, F., 25, 26, 63
Turner, B., 68
Turner, C. S. V., 62, 65–67, 71

U
Umemoto, K., 22

V
Valencia, R. R., 26, 41
Vargas, L., 64
Vasquez, P. L., 27
Vega, B. E., 27, 28, 31, 32
Vera, H., 67–69
Vilensky, M., 2
Villalpando, O., 20, 21, 27, 66, 67
Vizenor, G., 24

W
Walker, L., 61
Ward, L., 63
Web, C., 41
Wijeyesinghe, C. L., 84
Wilder, C. S., 25
Winant, H., 39, 40, 46, 85
Windchief, S. R., 22
Witham, K. A., 81
Wittenbrink, A. B., 69
Wood, F., 41
Wood, J. L., 66
Wooden, O. S., 50, 51
Woolf, S. H., 5
Wright, E. K., 22, 24
Wu, F. H., 19

Y
Yan, W., 62
Yosso, T. J., 16, 20, 21, 24–27, 30
Young, A., 63, 64

Z
Zia, H., 40
Zinn, H., 38

Subject Index

A

AANAPISI. *See* Asian American Native American and Pacific Islander Serving Institutions (AANAPISI)

Abstract liberalism, 47

Affirmative action debates, 54–57

Asian American Native American and Pacific Islander Serving Institutions (AANAPISI), 78

Asian Americans: annual income levels by ethnicity, 9; educational attainment levels by ethnicity, 7; living in poverty by ethnicity, 5

AsianCrit. *See* Asian critical race theory (AsianCrit)

Asian critical race theory (AsianCrit), 22–24; framework of, 23; scholarship, 22

Aversive racism, 84

B

Black-White paradigm, 19–20

Brown vs. Board of Education, 43

C

CECE model. *See* Culturally Engaging Campus Environments (CECE) model

Colorblind racism, 45–46, 84

Critical race theory (CRT), 17–28; Asian critical race theory, 22–24; Black-White paradigm, 19–20; Latina and Latino critical theory, 20–21; native Hawaiian critical theory, 24–25; and roles of racism in legal policy and practice, 18; scholarship, utility and limitations of, 25–28; tribal critical theory, 21–22

CRT. *See* Critical race theory (CRT)

CRT scholarship, 25–28

Cultural dissonance, 70

Culturally Engaging Campus Environments (CECE) model, 35–36; campus climate, 35; campus culture, 35; collectivist cultural orientations, 33; of college success, 32; cultural community service, 33; cultural familiarity, 32; culturally relevant knowledge, 32; culturally validating environments, 33; cultural relevance, 32–33; cultural responsiveness, 33; holistic support, 33; humanized educational environments, 33; meaningful cross-cultural engagement, 33; proactive philosophies, 33

Cultural racism, 47, 84

D

Differential racialization, 39

E

Equity Scorecard, 35–36

Ethnicity: annual Asian American income levels by, 9; Asian American educational attainment levels by, 7; Asian Americans living in poverty by, 5

F

Fisher vs. University of Texas at Austin, 3, 55, 57

G

Gratz vs. Bollinger, 55

I

Individual racism, 84
Institutional racism, 84

L

LatCrit. *See* Latina and Latino critical theory (LatCrit)
Latina and Latino critical theory (LatCrit), 20–21

M

Minoritized, 84

N

National Center for Education Statistics (NCES), 61
Native Hawaiian critical theory (KanakaCrit), 24–25
NCES. *See* National Center for Education Statistics (NCES)
Negroes in College, 17
Neoliberalism, 47

O

Oppression, 85

P

Poverty: United States population living in, by race, 4

R

Race: annual income levels by, 8; educational attainment levels by, 6; intercentricity of, 19; United States population living in poverty by, 4

Racial equity: on college campuses, 79–82; definition of, 13,85; in higher education policy, 77–79, in higher education scholarship, 75–77
Racial formation, 39, 85
Racial hostility,67–68; in classroom, 64–65
Racial invisibility and silencing, 69
Racialization, 39, 85
Racial justice advocacy: critical thinking about, 14; institutional framework for, 80
Racially conscious institutional models, 29–36; campus climate for diversity framework, 29–31; CECE model, 31–34; Equity Scorecard, 35–36; institutional diversity framework, 34–35
Racial marginalization, 66–67
Racial microaggressions, 45
Racial prejudice and stereotypes, 68–69
Racial resistance, to authority and expertise, 62–64
Racial scrutiny, of research agendas, 65–66
Racial segregation, 69–70
Racial taxation, from excess service, 66
Racial theory, in higher education; critical race theory, 17–28. *See also* Critical race theory (CRT); foundations of, 16–17
Racism: aversive, 84; color-blind, 45–46, 84; cultural, 47, 84; definition of, 83; in higher education. *See* Racism, in higher education; individual, 84; institutional, 84; secondhand, 85; in society. *See* Racism, in society; systemic, 85
Racism, in higher education, 10–13; in academic pipeline, 61–62; and affirmative action debates, 54–57; contradictory cultural pressures, 70–71; cultural dissonance, 70; and emerging policy issues, 59–60; experiences of faculty, 60–67; and finance, 57–59; as framework for understanding race, 10–13; hostility in classroom, 64–65; intercentricity of, 19; invisibility and silencing, 69; manifestations of, 49–60;

marginalization and isolation, 66–67, 71; in policies, 52; prejudice and stereotypes, 68–69; resistance to authority and expertise, 62–64; role in experiences of college students, 67–71; scrutiny of research agendas, 65–66; segregation, 69–70; and standardized testing, 53–54; systemic, 49–71, 80–81; taxation from excess service, 66

Racism, in society: abstract liberalism, 47; color-blind, 45–46; cultural, 47; differential racialization, 39; forms of, 44–48; historical foundations of, 38–44; minimization of, 47; naturalization, 47; neoliberalism, 47; racial formation, 39; racialization, 39

Racism Without Racists, 47

Regents of the University of California *vs.* Bakke, 54

S

Schuette vs. Coalition to Defend Affirmative Action, 56

Secondhand racism, 85

Symbolic racism. *See* Aversive racism

Systemic racism, 49–71, 80–81, 85

T

TribalCrit. *See* Tribal critical theory (TribalCrit)

Tribal critical theory (TribalCrit), 21–22; features of, 21; TribalCrit scholars *vs.* LatCrit scholars, 20

U

UCLA. *See* University of California, Los Angeles (UCLA)

UIUC. *See* University of Illinois, Urbana–Champaign (UIUC)

University of California, Los Angeles (UCLA), 2

University of Illinois, Urbana–Champaign (UIUC), 2–3

V

Vicarious racism. *See* Secondhand racism

W

White supremacy, 86

About the Authors

Samuel D. Museus, PhD, is associate professor of higher education and student affairs and serves as director of the Culturally Engaging Campus Environments (CECE) Project at Indiana University, Bloomington. His research agenda focuses on diversity and equity in higher education, institutional environments, and success among diverse student populations in college. He has produced over 150 publications and conference presentations on the factors that influence educational outcomes among diverse populations and received several national awards for his scholarship.

María C. Ledesma, PhD, is assistant professor in the Department of Educational Leadership & Policy at the University of Utah's College of Education. Her research interests include equity oriented critical policy analysis, including the history and application of race-conscious social policy in higher education. A first-generation college student, Dr. Ledesma earned her PhD in education from the University of California, Los Angeles. As a doctoral student, she served as 32nd Student Regent for the University of California, the first Latina to hold this post.

Tara L. Parker, PhD, is associate professor of higher education and chair of the Leadership in Education Department at the University of Massachusetts Boston. Her research focuses on access and equity in higher education, with an emphasis on how policy impacts students of color and other historically underrepresented groups. She is author of *The State of Developmental Education: Higher Education and Public Policy Priorities* (Palgrave MacMillan, 2014).

About the ASHE Higher Education Report Series

Since 1983, the ASHE (formerly ASHE-ERIC) Higher Education Report Series has been providing researchers, scholars, and practitioners with timely and substantive information on the critical issues facing higher education. Each monograph presents a definitive analysis of a higher education problem or issue, based on a thorough synthesis of significant literature and institutional experiences. Topics range from planning to diversity and multiculturalism, to performance indicators, to curricular innovations. The mission of the Series is to link the best of higher education research and practice to inform decision making and policy. The reports connect conventional wisdom with research and are designed to help busy individuals keep up with the higher education literature. Authors are scholars and practitioners in the academic community. Each report includes an executive summary, review of the pertinent literature, descriptions of effective educational practices, and a summary of key issues to keep in mind to improve educational policies and practice.

This series is one of the most peer reviewed in higher education. A National Advisory Board made up of ASHE members reviews proposals. A National Review Board of ASHE scholars and practitioners reviews completed manuscripts. Six monographs are published each year, and they are approximately 144 pages in length. The reports are widely disseminated through Jossey-Bass and John Wiley & Sons, and they are available online to subscribing institutions through Wiley Online Library (http://wileyonlinelibrary.com).

Call for Proposals

The ASHE Higher Education Report Series is actively looking for proposals. We encourage you to contact one of the editors, Dr. Kelly Ward (kaward@wsu.edu) or Dr. Lisa Wolf-Wendel (lwolf@ku.edu), with your ideas.

Recent Titles

Volume 41 ASHE Higher Education Report

1. Revenue Generation Strategies: Leveraging Higher Education Resources for Increased Income
   Jeffrey W. Alstete
2. Public Policy and Higher Education: Strategies for Framing a Research Agenda
   Nicholas W. Hillman, David A. Tandberg, Brain A. Sponsler
3. Critical Race Theory in Higher Education: 20 Years of Theoretical and Research Innovations
   Dorian L. McCoy, Dirk J. Rodricks
4. Affirmative Action at a Crossroads: *Fisher* and Forward
   Edna Chun, Alvin Evans
5. The "Front Porch": Examining the Increasing Interconnection of University and Athletic Department Funding
   Jordan R. Bass, Claire C. Schaeperkoetter, Kyle S. Bunds
6. Parent and Family Engagement in Higher Education
   Judy Marquez Kiyama, Casandra E. Harper, with Delma Ramos, David Aguayo, Laura A. Page, Kathy Adams Riester

Volume 40 ASHE Higher Education Report

1. Asian Americans in Higher Education: Charting New Realities
   Yoon K. Pak, Dina C. Maramba, and Xavier J. Hernandez
2. Community University Engagement: A Process for Building Democratic Communities
   Tami L. Moore
3. Black Male Collegians: Increasing Access, Retention, and Persistence in Higher Education
   Robert T. Palmer, J. Luke Wood, T. Elon Dancy II, and Terrell L. Strayhorn
4. Representing "U": Popular Culture, Media, and Higher Education
   Pauline J. Reynolds
5. Part-Time on the Tenure Track
   Joan M. Herbers
6. Student Engagement Online: What Works and Why
   Katrina A. Meyer

Volume 39 ASHE Higher Education Report

1. Latinos in Higher Education and Hispanic-Serving Institutions: Creating Conditions for Success
   Anne-Marie Núñez, Richard E. Hoover, Kellie Pickett, A. Christine Stuart-Carruthers, and Maria Vázquez
2. Performance Funding for Higher Education: What Are the Mechanisms? What Are the Impacts?
   Kevin J. Dougherty and Vikash Reddy
3. Understanding Institutional Diversity in American Higher Education
   Michael S. Harris
4. Cultivating Leader Identity and Capacity in Students from Diverse Backgrounds
   Kathy L. Guthrie, Tamara Bertrand Jones, Laura Osteen, and Shouping Hu

ASHE HIGHER EDUCATION REPORT

ORDER FORM SUBSCRIPTION AND SINGLE ISSUES

DISCOUNTED BACK ISSUES:

Use this form to receive 20% off all back issues of *ASHE Higher Education Report*.
All single issues priced at **$23.20** (normally $29.00)

TITLE	ISSUE NO.	ISBN
_____	_____	_____
_____	_____	_____
_____	_____	_____

*Call 1-800-835-6770 or see mailing instructions below. When calling, mention the promotional code JBNND
to receive your discount. For a complete list of issues, please visit www.josseybass.com/go/aehe*

SUBSCRIPTIONS: (1 YEAR, 6 ISSUES)

☐ New Order ☐ Renewal

U.S.	☐ Individual: $174	☐ Institutional: $352
CANADA/MEXICO	☐ Individual: $174	☐ Institutional: $412
ALL OTHERS	☐ Individual: $210	☐ Institutional: $463

Call 1-800-835-6770 or see mailing and pricing instructions below.
Online subscriptions are available at www.onlinelibrary.wiley.com

ORDER TOTALS:

Issue / Subscription Amount: $ _____

Shipping Amount: $ _____
(for single issues only – subscription prices include shipping)

Total Amount: $ _____

SHIPPING CHARGES:

First Item	$6.00
Each Add'l Item	$2.00

*(No sales tax for U.S. subscriptions. Canadian residents, add GST for subscription orders. Individual rate subscriptions must
be paid by personal check or credit card. Individual rate subscriptions may not be resold as library copies.)*

BILLING & SHIPPING INFORMATION:

☐ **PAYMENT ENCLOSED:** *(U.S. check or money order only. All payments must be in U.S. dollars.)*

☐ **CREDIT CARD:** ☐ VISA ☐ MC ☐ AMEX

Card number _____Exp. Date_____

Card Holder Name_____Card Issue # _____

Signature _____Day Phone_____

☐ **BILL ME:** *(U.S. institutional orders only. Purchase order required.)*

Purchase order # _____
Federal Tax ID 13559302 • GST 89102-8052

Name_____

Address_____

Phone_____ E-mail_____

Copy or detach page and send to: **John Wiley & Sons, One Montgomery Street, Suite 1000,
San Francisco, CA 94104-4594**

Order Form can also be faxed to: **888-481-2665**

PROMO JBNND